THE AMERICAN MENTAL HEALTH FOUNDATION
ASTOR SERVICES STUDY

EARLY IDENTIFICATION, PALLIATIVE CARE, AND PREVENTION OF PSYCHOTIC DISORDERS IN CHILDREN AND YOUTH

Mary Nichols, Suzanne Button, Katherine Hoople, and Laura Lappan

2016

AMHF

AMERICAN MENTAL HEALTH FOUNDATION BOOKS

American Mental Health Foundation Inc
128 Second Place Garden Suite
Brooklyn New York 11231-4102

americanmentalhealthfoundation.org

Library of Congress Cataloging-in-Publication Data

Names: Nichols, Mary (Mary C.), author. | Button, Suzanne, author. | Hoople, Katherine, author. | Lappan, Laura, author. | American Mental Health Foundation, issuing body.
Title: Early identification, palliative care, and prevention of psychotic disorders in children and youth / Mary Nichols, Suzanne Button, Katherine Hoople, and Laura Lappan.
Description: Brooklyn, New York : American Mental Health Foundation Books, 2016. | Includes bibliographical references.
Identifiers: LCCN 2015041485 (print) | LCCN 2015043869 (ebook) | ISBN 978-1-935307-31-0 (hardcover) | ISBN 9781590565407 (ebook)
Subjects: | MESH: Child—Case Reports. | Psychotic Disorders—diagnosis—Case Reports. | Psychotic Disorders—therapy—Case Reports. | Adolescent—Case Reports.
Classification: LCC RJ503 (print) | LCC RJ503 (ebook) | NLM WS 350 | DDC 616.8900835—dc23
LC record available at http://lccn.loc.gov/2015041485

All identifying information in the case histories discussed has been omitted to the extent possible.

Contents

Publisher's foreword

As the present book is issued, The American Mental Health Foundation reaches upward and grows toward 100 years of philanthropic work. AMHF is dedicated to the welfare of people suffering from emotional problems, with a particular concern for at-risk youth, individuals of any age with special needs, and elders. Historically, AMHF devoted its efforts to bettering quality of treatment, and developing more effective methods, making all of this available to lower-income wage earners. Today, the mission of AMHF lies in three areas: research, publishing, and educational seminars/Webinars.

Since inception as one of the first nonprofit foundations of its kind, AMHF has been a pioneering force in research and advocacy. Its major therapeutic advances and improved training methods are described in several publications: the three-part series The Search for the Future. Two of these books are available on the AMHF Web site under the titles *The Challenge for Group Psychotherapy* (volume 1) and *The Challenge for Psychoanalysis and Psychotherapy: Solutions for the Future* (volume 2). Portions of these books are also reprinted on the AMHF Web site in French and German. Volume 3, originally issued in 2000, is available from AMHF Books in traditional and e-book formats: *Crucial Choices—Crucial Changes: The Resurrection of Psychotherapy.*

AMHF Books has been an exciting venture since it was launched in late 2009. In addition to *Crucial Choices—Crucial Changes,* it includes eight titles by Dr. Raymond B. Flannery Jr., Associate Professor of Psychology, Department of Psychiatry (Part Time), Harvard Medical School, one of the authorities on posttraumatic stress disorder (PTSD), the most recent being *Violence—Why People Do Bad Things, with Strategies to Reduce that Risk;* four classic books (two reissued, two posthumously published) by Erich Fromm; *Live Your Dreams, Change the World: The Psychology of Personal Fulfillment for Women* by Drs. Joanne H. Gavin, James Campbell Quick, and David J. Gavin; and four by Dr. Henry Kellerman: *Group Psychotherapy and Personality; Personality: How It Forms; Anatomy of Delusion;* and *There's No Handle on My Door: Stories of Patients in Mental Hospitals.*

The present book is a collaborative effort: researched by Astor Services for Children & Families, funded by The American Mental Health Foundation. It presents the significant findings of a two-year study with wider implications and potential applications. Since 1953, Astor Services (formerly The Astor Home for Children) has been providing behavioral and educational services in a caring environment wherein children and their families find strength, healing, hope, and trust. Astor Services reach more than seven-thousand children and families every year in thirty-two locations in the Hudson Valley of New York State and the Bronx.

* * *

The costs of promoting and conducting research, organizing seminars and Webinars, and disseminating the findings in fulfillment of the mission of AMHF are high. All donations, made via PayPal on the foundation Web site, or posted to the address listed on the copyright page of this book, constitute a meaningful contribution to the public good. If your commitment is deeper, consider partnering with AMHF in the form of a legacy bequest, so that the foundation would continue to serve society for another 100 years. We thank you for your interest in the present book and for helping AMHF build a more compassionate society. Please discover our work in greater detail on the Web site:

americanmentalhealthfoundation.org

Acknowledgments

The authors would like to thank the agency staff, whose exceptional, compassionate work with youth and families helped guide and shape our work and knowledge.

This project would not have been possible without the generosity of The American Mental Health Foundation, Inc., and this monograph would not have been produced without the guidance of William Van Ornum, PhD, FAPA.

For consultation about best practices for early intervention in psychosis, we thank Michael Leo Birnbaum, MD, Assistant Professor, Hofstra North Shore-LIJ School of Medicine and Lisa Dixon, MD, MPH, Director, Center for Practice Innovations, New York State Psychiatric Institute.

For training and consultation regarding assessment of psychosis risk, we thank Barbara C. Walsh, PhD, Clinical Coordinator for the PRIME Clinic at Yale University School of Medicine.

For implementation support in cognitive skills training with C8 Sciences, we thank Bruce E. Wexler, MD, Professor Emeritus of Psychiatry and Senior Research Scientist at Yale School of Medicine and Greg Skinner, Director of Field Operations at C8 Sciences.

Lastly, and most importantly, we extend our deepest gratitude to the youth and families who participated in this project. We asked them to share of their struggles and successes in the face of significant personal challenges and by doing so help our field learn more about effective care. They gave us a window on what it is like to live with, or be a caregiver to, a young person with a serious mental illness. We are honored to learn from them and to privilege their voices in this work.

CHAPTER ONE

Background on psychosis risk and development

This chapter reviews the problem of psychosis and psychosis risk in youth, including information from the scientific literature about risk factors that predict conversion to full-blown psychotic disorders like schizophrenia. Studies suggest that the combined presence of genetic risk, a recent and dramatic deterioration in functioning, unusual thought content, social impairment, and a history of substance abuse are highly predictive of psychosis (Cannon et al, 2008).

Schizophrenia and other psychotic disorders are primarily thought of as a problem experienced by adults, but are also seen in children and adolescents. This spectrum of disorders is among the most debilitating in terms of human suffering and cost to society and often follows a lifelong course. An individual who develops a psychotic disorder typically shows a prodromal syndrome (or "prodrome") prior to the first psychotic break, which usually occurs in late adolescence or early adulthood. Temporally, the prodrome is defined as the period between the time the first noticeable change in functioning occurs and the onset of frank psychosis. A pattern of prodromal symptoms is demonstrated in 75 percent of individuals who eventually develop full-blown psychosis (Häfner and an der Heiden, 1997). There has been a significant effort in recent research to describe this phase of illness in terms of how many experience it, its length, and which symptoms are most commonly observed (e.g., Shioiri, Shinada, Kuwabara, and Someya, 2007; van Kampen, 2005).

With the goal of developing early identification and prevention strategies, researchers have sought to learn more about what happens in the time before the transition to a full-blown psychotic disorder. Corcoran et al (2003) conducted a qualitative study of the evolution of symptoms in which parents of prodromal adolescents were interviewed. Analysis of thematic content revealed two subgroups, "declining" and "never normal," with the individuals noted to be "declining" showing a higher rate of conversion to psychosis. A stage model of transition to schizophrenia, proposed by Maier, Cornblatt, and Merikangas (2003), includes four phases: (1) the premorbid phase with risk factors for psychosis but no psychosocial dysfunction; (2) the early prodromal phase with affective and negative symptoms and psychosocial impairment; (3) the late prodromal phase with attenuated psychotic symptoms; and (4) the final psychosis phase. During the prodrome, symptoms are seen that are not specific to psychosis such as mood disturbance, anxiety, social withdrawal, and changes in sleep and appetite. Additionally, signs of thought disorder might emerge including unusual ideas, thought blocking, and subjective disruption in self-perception (Norman, Scholten, Malla, and Ballageer, 2005).

In recent years there has been an intensified effort to create models of risk that can reliably predict conversion to a full-blown psychotic disorder, e.g., schizophrenia. In a multisite longitudinal study conducted with youth in North America, and funded by the National Institute of Mental Health (NIMH), specific factors were identified to predict the development of a psychotic disorder (Cannon et al, 2008). The researchers used the Structured Interview for Prodromal Symptoms (SIPS; McGlashan, Walsh, and Woods, 2010) criteria with patients who were seeking treatment and followed up with them over two-and-a-half years. The rate of conversion to a psychotic disorder was 35 percent; however, when two or three out of the five unique factors below were present at the baseline assessment the risk of conversion elevated to between 68 and 80 percent:

(1a) Genetic risk for schizophrenia *and*
(1b) Recent deterioration in functioning
(2) Highly unusual thought content
(3) Social impairment
(4) History of substance abuse.

This predictive power, at a level of accuracy that is comparable to what can predict major medical illnesses, is invaluable to practitioners seeking to identify patients at risk and implement prevention and early intervention efforts. The recent research is promising, and more studies are urgently needed to build the evidence base regarding indicators of risk, prevention strategies, and approaches to intervene rapidly with children and adolescents at risk for psychotic disorders. In a review of the literature by Correll, Hauser, Auther, and Cornblatt (2010), the current evidence and directions for future research were discussed. The authors called for further inquiry into the validity of psychosis risk indicators and predictors of outcomes via studies that have the potential to inform clinical practice directly.

More in-depth studies of individual risk factors further elucidate the predictive impact of each set of variables:

Genetic risk—Family, twin, and adoption studies suggest a strong genetic component for schizophrenia such that lifetime risk is five-to-twenty times higher in first-degree relatives. In addition, genetic and environmental factors interact, thereby shaping neurodevelopmental processes and affecting illness risk and progression (McClellan, Stock, and American Academy of Child and Adolescent Psychiatry (AACAP) Committee on Quality Issues (CQI), 2013).

Highly unusual thought content—Unusual-thought content, especially attenuated-positive symptoms and behaviors in children such as illusions, ideas of reference, and magical thinking continue to be strong predictive indicators in more recent diagnosis and treatment updates (Lachman, 2014). In fact, Woodberry and colleagues (2014) conducted research suggesting that childhood onset of delusions, suspiciousness, and other abnormalities may be even more common than previously thought, with reported recall of these psychotic-like experiences occurring at a rate of 23 percent for individuals with a high risk for developing a psychotic disorder.

Social impairment—Aiming to examine the relationship between social-functioning problems and psychosis in adolescents, researchers sought to determine whether poor social functioning tends to present before psychosis emerges and thus is truly a risk factor, or that emerging psychotic symptoms cause social impairment, which then results in further progression of psychosis (Sullivan, Lewis, Wiles, Thompson, and Evans, 2013). Results indicate that social problems, specifically with peers, persisted but did not worsen during middle and late childhood and early adolescence for those youth who developed psychosis.

History of substance abuse—Researchers have learned that broadly defined substance-abuse history puts youth at risk for psychosis, and moreover there appears to be a specific link with cannabis. Considered together with other genetic and environmental-risk factors, Goerke and Kumra (2013) suggest in their comprehensive review of the relevant literature that adolescents abusing cannabis have an increased vulnerability for developing psychosis.

This study was fueled by the authors' collective belief that practice-based research has the potential to contribute a great deal to the field because it is embedded in real-world practice settings. We developed the program evaluation and quality improvement project described in this study to explore the risk factors discussed above—previously elucidated in academic research—in real-world services for youth who present in the community with serious mental-health concerns. Our agency, Astor Services, is uniquely suited to conduct this study as a provider of the full spectrum of behavioral-health services to marginalized, socioeconomically diverse youth. With the generous support of The American Mental Health Foundation (AMHF), we were simultaneously able to explore the risk factors identified in the research and conclusively provide a more comprehensive, high-quality evaluation service for youth in the Astor treatment programs.

CHAPTER TWO

Current practices for evaluation and intervention strategies for psychosis in youth

Despite the high prevalence of mental disorders across the globe, health and behavioral health systems have lagged in their ability to provide accessible, effective care for individuals suffering from psychiatric disturbance (McCrone et al, 2013). One compelling explanation for this lag lies in the gap between what those struggling with mental disorders need (closeness to home, brief, targeted treatment that supports functioning) and what services actually are available. Individuals, particularly youth, who receive public mental-health care often receive fragmented, ineffective services, and their service provision is further disrupted when they turn eighteen and are transferred to the adult-service provision system (Osgood et al, 2010).

This state of affairs is particularly disturbing with regard to youth struggling with, or at risk for, psychotic disturbance.

Individuals with psychosis can live stable, productive lives with appropriate support and treatment. However, the decision to seek and remain engaged with mental-health treatment is strongly related to one's experiences with treatment in first and early contacts with the system (Munson et al, 2012). The more collaborative, supportive, and salient to the client treatment contacts are, the more likely that youth will access the mental-health service system as needed across the life span (Pescosolido, 2011). If youth experience ineffective, noncollaborative, nonsalient care (e.g., psychodynamic therapy for a youth who needs functional skill-building and prevocational support), they are likely to stay away from the mental-health system until an acute crisis brings them back.

This chapter clarifies current practices used in behavioral health care for youth presenting with symptoms of psychosis and psychosis-risk. Care as usual typically involves participation in a standard initial assessment during which information about youth needs and strengths is used to formulate a care plan that addresses the presenting problems. A wide range of activities can be targeted in the care plan, including interventions related to psychotherapy, skills training, medication management, case management, and educational interventions. However, specialized and evidence-based assessment protocols to identify youth at risk of psychotic episodes are underutilized, and youth generally receive a standard package of individual and/or group and/or family therapy as well as psychiatric services. Clinicians have little opportunity to conduct further comprehensive evaluations with individual youth that present with risk for psychosis. The types of interventions that are most effective with these youth—those that are collaboratively planned with families, coordinate care provided across multiple settings (e.g., home, school, therapy office, psychiatrist's office), and are focused on building skills for optimal functioning—are infrequently delivered.

However, ample support exists for the effectiveness of a collaborative, "chronic care" model of treatment that emphasizes integration of multiple disciplines with empowered, educated, and actively involved patients (Croghan and Brown, 2010). Functional and collaborative evaluation leading to a collaboratively designed menu of treatments such as community or contextual interventions, vocational or educational consultation, training or support, cognitive behavioral therapy, family support and skill building, youth social-skills training, and physical-health improvement tend to lead to better long term outcomes for those facing chronic psychotic disturbance (Dixon et al, 2010).

Put simply, providers must be able to contextualize treatment protocols to the unique needs and circumstances of those facing psychotic symptoms, educate their patients about and use evidence-based treatments in these protocols, and engage youth, their families, and their educational and community contexts in the application of these protocols. Yet many young people facing psychosis do not receive this contextualized care. At the present time, despite the prevalence of psychosis risk and symptoms in youth and young adults (as high as 13 percent in some studies), only about 15 clinics that specialize in this kind of targeted care exist in the United States (Internet Mental Health Initiative, 2010), and they are widely geographically dispersed (Calkins et al, 2014).

Large, multisite federally funded programs of research have been underway during the last decade to develop and study outcomes for specialized programs to treat youngsters and young adults experiencing early phase psychosis. For example, there is an initiative called the Recovery After an Initial Schizophrenia Episode Project's Early Treatment Program (RAISE-ETP). In one study with this cohort, researchers were interested in learning about prescription practices in a real world clinic setting and whether best practices were being used by prescribers, such as starting antipsychotic medications at a low dose and increasing dosage slowly (Robinson et al, 2014). Findings suggest that actual practices are more similar to practices used among patients with chronic schizophrenia-spectrum disorders, wherein higher dosages are given initially and increased more rapidly in almost 40 percent of patients. Health-insurance status, race, and ethnicity factors were linked with prescribing patterns that were more divergent from best practices. The authors concluded that there is a need for education to prescribers about best practices, and furthermore that policy makers should be made aware of service-delivery factors that may impact the quality of care received by first-episode patients in community clinics.

Another study looked at feasibility and effectiveness of a treatment service provided to individuals with early phase psychosis at a university-affiliated community mental health clinic via a pragmatic randomized controlled trial (Srihari et al, 2014). The clinic for Specialized Treatment Early in Psychosis (STEP) was designed to deliver care that is coordinated, collaborative, and comprehensive in nature, using a multidisciplinary-team approach. Patients and their families were given the opportunity to select which types of services they needed from options that included cognitive-behavioral therapy, medications, family education, and case management to support educational and employment goals. Compared to patients who received outpatient treatment as usual, after one year the individuals who participated in the step program had fewer and shorter hospitalizations and improved community functioning. These positive outcomes were achieved in a clinic operating in "the real world" of complex, fragmented health care and in the face of challenges to provide treatment that is low-cost and effective. Srihari and colleagues (2014) also found that their participants had on average experienced psychotic symptoms for almost a year before accessing needed services, and it was noted that this is a typical duration of untreated illness in this population.

The barriers to effective care for youth with sub-psychotic or psychotic disturbance are significant. Careful, thorough, functional evaluation is a must for these youth, and the time and expertise needed to conduct such an evaluation often is lacking in resource-strapped youth mental-health programs. Lower quality, less-accessible services are a ubiquitous problem in mental health, and the high degree of skill and expertise required to treat and prevent psychosis effectively is rare in the mental-health service system (McGorry, 2012).

When the consequences of inadequate care for serious mental illness in youth are reviewed, the case for action supporting contextualized care is only strengthened. Well-replicated studies suggest that better mental health for youth reduces risk for school failure, sexual risk-taking, suicide, substance abuse; and reduces the long-term likelihood of incarceration, unemployment, and health problems (see for example Aos et al, 2004). For youth with psychotic disturbance, effective care can intervene on the path to potentially violent behaviors (Winsper et al, 2013), whereas an absence of appropriate intervention can lead to long term cognitive deficits and their attendant social and functional problems (Chang et al, 2013).

The challenge of providing contextualized, collaborative care to youth with psychotic disturbance can be met by combining promising, wrap-around service models for youth (see for example Winters et al, 2009) and comprehensive, recovery-oriented approaches for early intervention with psychosis (cf. RAISE-ETP). Wrap-around services are developed collaboratively with youth and family to target client-driven needs, and are focused on functional and interpersonal success. The "treatment team" is led, in part, by the family and youth, and treatment planning consists of choosing from a menu of evidence-based and best practices to meet the family's needs, and recognize their resources and right to make choices. Recovery-oriented approaches for psychosis risk also emphasize collaboration, choice, and functional outcomes with an enhanced focus on peer support and appropriate pharmacological treatment.

In this study, we aim to develop a model that combines these two approaches and to test its applicability and success in the provision of adequate, early intervention for psychosis risk.

CHAPTER THREE

Development and implementation of *The American Mental Health Foundation Early Identification for Psychosis Project*

Following is an overview of the conception and implementation of the project in collaboration with program leadership and treatment providers at select Astor programs. The specific methodological design of the project included screening for empirically supported risk factors, the use of structured and specialized evaluation tools developed by experts in the field of psychosis identification, as well as collaborative skills and strengths-based treatment redesign and follow-up.

These tools allowed the project team to attend to issues that might be missed in care as usual, such as specificity of symptoms, diagnostic complexity, and barriers to accessing potentially helpful interventions. Subsequently, we offered in consultation with families and care providers, a more fine-grained understanding of each youth, which allowed us to place youth on a path to receive individualized, evidence-based interventions. Additionally, we aimed to systematically measure impact on youth functioning over time, assist with implementing the interventions planned, and continued to evaluate outcomes in a seamless process. Brief case examples are given to illustrate the clinical relevance of the comprehensive evaluation and overarching goal of engaging families in a collaborative, empowering, and strengths-based approach.

PROJECT CONCEPTION

Children and youth receiving services in the agency's diverse treatment programs typically participate in a standard initial assessment during which information about their needs and strengths is used to formulate a care plan. A clinician working within the structure of these programs has, at most, 90 minutes to meet the family and youth for the first time, identify treatment needs, and formulate a care plan that addresses the presenting problems. There is little opportunity to use the assessment data collected to screen youth for risk of developing specific problems (such as psychosis) and conduct in-depth, structured, diagnostic evaluations of youth. Although the agency engages in continuous quality-improvement initiatives, and routinely collects data to inform program development and measure the clinical outcomes of services, we rarely use data to identify specific clients who might need specialized early intervention. There are limited means available to work with data in this proactive approach, which would involve the implementation of rapid data collection, review, and feedback process in an already resource-strapped healthcare-delivery system. Instead, data primarily are used to evaluate clinical treatment outcomes in the aggregate, or minimally at the service area or program level.

At the time of conception of the project, there was a growing interest in finding innovative ways to use data to drive clinical decision-making at the individual client level. Our team wanted to explore how we could use data collected routinely (and without additional burden on busy clinicians), to create an identifying algorithm for youth at risk for, or already experiencing, psychotic disorders. We then sought to impact the lives of these youth directly by providing a consultative assessment and technical assistance protocol designed to give families, treatment providers, and other collaterals (as needed), the information and support required to implement best practices. We also actively solicited feedback from the clinicians and program leaders about what they thought was needed from the project in terms of knowledge, technical assistance, or support. For example, when we heard that clinicians were unable to attend meetings with school staff, we offered families our services to write letters or attend in the clinician's place to advocate for each youth's needs as they pertained to the goals of the project. This was not something we could have anticipated at the start, but if we had not listened to and prioritized this concern we would not have been privileging the voice of the most important stakeholders in the process—the service recipients.

PROJECT TIMELINE

Generous project funding from The American Mental Health Foundation began in October 2012, when the project was staffed, the research design approved, and the screening and comprehensive-evaluation procedures as well as the consultation menu of evidence-based interventions were developed. Staff training on the structured interview protocol was completed, and by June 2013 hundreds of agency youth were screened for psychosis-risk factors. Participant recruitment began in March 2013, comprehensive evaluations began in April 2013, and the first consultation meeting was held in May 2013, with follow-up data collection beginning in June 2013. In winter 2013-14, participant enrollment was closed. All evaluations were completed by January 2014, and consultations were finished in March 2014. Outcomes for all thirteen project youth were tracked for one year post-consultation, so that the last follow-up data collection occurred in March 2015.

Below, is described the screening procedure in more detail, our rationale for using it, and our evaluation of its effectiveness in identifying youth at risk for psychosis.

THE SCREENING PROCEDURE

A numerical summary of youth screened and identified is seen (figure 1). Youth were determined to screen positive for psychosis risk if they had at least two of the risk factors shown in the literature to predict development of psychotic disorders:

genetic risk/family history with concurrent recent deterioration in functioning, unusual thought content or suspicion/paranoia, social impairment, or history of substance abuse (Cannon et al., 2008). We used the Child and Adolescent Needs and Strengths-NY (CANS-NY; Lyons, 2011) as the first step in our screening procedure, as it is used widely in the Astor services programs for a treatment-planning and outcomes-measurement tool. This structured assessment, widely used by professionals working with children and youth around the world, evaluates child/youth and family strengths and needs across broad domains: Child/Youth Strengths, Primary Caregiver Strengths, Primary Caregiver Needs, Child/Youth Life Functioning, Child/Youth Risk Behaviors, and Child/Youth Behavioral Health. We included CANS-NY items that assess psychotic symptoms, social functioning, and substance abuse in the algorithm developed to identifty at-risk youth relevant to the study.

Youth who had a CANS-NY assessment within one year of recruitment, who were currently enrolled in one of the clinical-treatment programs of the agency, and who were between the ages of 8 and 17, were deemed eligible for initial project screening. Youth were from low to low-average SES families, and exhibited a range of levels of academic achievement. Three-hundred-sixty of the approximately 5,000 youth in care at the start of this project met these initial eligibility criteria. Of these 360, 74 screened positive using risk factor-related CANS-NY items. During the screening process, 25 youth were discharged from participating treatment programs. The 49 youth remaining received complete chart reviews. Of those reviewed, 38 youth met full eligibility criteria for participation in the study (positive initial CANS-NY screening on risk factors plus confirmation of at least three risk factors through chart review).

Once this initial group of potential subject youth was identified, our team visited participant program sites and educated clinical staff about the risk factors for psychosis. After reviewing lists of youth who had screened positive through our review, we asked for additional direct referrals from clinicians to identify any youth who may have been missed in our screening process. Clinical staff members were allowed ongoing referral access for the first nine months of the project, and with the addition of these referrals we fully screened 81 clients via the CANS and chart-review process. Positive risk for psychosis was confirmed for 64 of these clients and project staff began recruitment with a goal of enrolling as many of these youth as possible. However, because of a variety of reasons (e.g., family declined to participate due to lack of interest, client in hospital during recruitment attempts, client discharged from agency program during recruitment period, family unable to be reached by research team), 14 youth were enrolled in the project. One youth dropped out after completing the evaluation, and another youth dropped out during the follow-up phase because she was unable to be reached after being discharged from the agency program during the follow-up period. *All-in-all, a total of 12 youth fully completed the project.*

Figure 1: A numerical summary of screening and recruitment of youth

- We started with 5,000 (approx.) total youth in care across the agency
- 360 out of approximately 5,000 youth (7.2 percent) met initial project eligibility (in care at a selected program, between 8 and 17 years old)
- 74 of those 360 youth (20.56 percent) screened positive using CANS-only screening
- 49 of those 74 youth (66.2 percent) received chart reviews (25 had been discharged from care)
- 32 clients were directly referred by Agency clinicians and received chart reviews
- 64 of those 81 youth (79.01 percent) screened positive for psychosis risk with the CANS and chart-review process
- 12 of the 64 youth (18.7 percent) who fully screened positive completed the project

EVALUATION OF PSYCHOSIS SCREENING PROCEDURE

To explore differences between youth enrolled in the project and youth receiving care as usual in the Agency's other treatment programs, we compared three distinct groups: (1) 14 enrolled project youth, (2) 67 at-risk youth who met the initial assessment criteria but not the in-depth evaluation and diagnosis criteria for enrollment in the project (the screened youth), and (3) the general population of youth served in the Agency (the Agency youth). Youth were considered to be at risk for psychosis if they had at least two of the risk factors (thought-disturbance, genetic risk with recent deterioration of functioning, social impairment, and substance-abuse history; Cannon et al, 2008). The mean number of risk factors for psychosis for project youth was 2.43 whereas for screened youth it was 2.04, indicating that those enrolled in the study showed greater risk.

With the intent of highlighting the differences and similarities among the three groups, we provide some data from the Child and Adolescent Needs and Strengths (CANS) used for the screening. Specifically, CANS items used for screening purposes were chosen based on their similarities to the risk factors known in the literature to predict conversion to full psychotic disorders in youth. Items assessing symptoms of Psychosis, Substance Use, and impairment in Social Functioning were selected.

In the chart, CANS scores range from 0 to 3 such that higher scores indicate better functioning. As can be seen, the project youth generally evinced lower functioning compared to the other groups, especially on behavioral health CANS items. These data suggest that the screening procedures appropriately identified youth with psychosis risk. They also illustrate that a CANS-only screening process did not adequately differentiate among youth at risk for psychosis – note that the scores for the screened and project youth were essentially the same. Hence, a more in-depth evaluation and diagnosis was indicated in order to identify effectively youth at risk for psychosis.

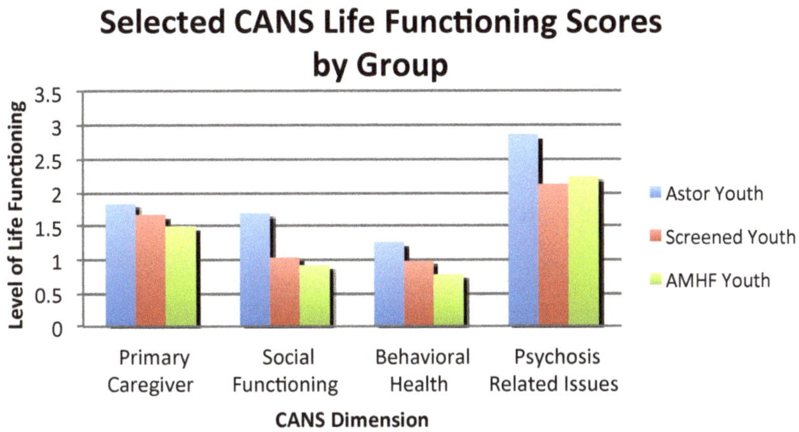

RECRUITMENT OF YOUTH AND STAFF ENGAGEMENT IN THE PROJECT

To make our recruitment efforts targeted and efficient, we conducted visits of programs and met with staff to educate them about psychosis in youth and facilitate engagement with the project. This was an especially important aspect of the implementation – making the project relevant to the daily work of service provision, and encouraging clinicians to help identify and reach out to youth and families who were likely to benefit from participating. At these visits, we shared with clinicians and supervisors their clients' screening results, and initiated a conversation with them about their clinical work with these youth and families. We asked if the results made sense to them, and when youth had screened positive for psychosis risk we encouraged clinicians to discuss concerns about symptoms and functioning in more detail. This data and functioning review dovetailed nicely into a discussion of how to engage youth and their families in the project, consideration of how it might be helpful to have a comprehensive evaluation of psychosis risk and diagnosis, needs and strengths, a review of the current approach to treatment, and consultation about evidence-based practices that could be added to the youth's care plan.

In many of the programs, upon learning about the project clinicians began to refer their clients directly to us for participation. We completed the screening process (including a chart review) and shared psychosis-risk results with the clinicians. When it had been collaboratively decided that a young person was a good candidate for the project, we asked clinicians to initiate contact with the identified youth and their families and to obtain consent to refer to the project. Once clinicians confirmed families had consented, we called each family to discuss possible participation, and to schedule a meeting to administer signed informed consent and begin the comprehensive evaluation. We structured the recruitment conversations with a prepared, semi-structured script that ensured key points were covered (such as risks, benefits, and the voluntary nature of participation).

COMPREHENSIVE EVALUATION

The comprehensive evaluation was conducted over a range of between one and three sessions depending on the youth, each lasting about two hours in total. The evaluation included the semi-structured interviews and assessments described below.

SCHEDULE FOR AFFECTIVE DISORDERS AND SCHIZOPHRENIA FOR SCHOOL-AGE CHILDREN (K-SADS-PL)

The K-SADS-PL is a semi-structured interview that aims to assess psychopathology in children and adolescents up to age eighteen. Upon administration of this diagnostic interview, a trained clinician can determine whether a youth has met criteria in the past or currently for a variety of DSM disorders. Specific probes and descriptions of criteria are included in the instrument and can be used as guiding questions in order to gather the pertinent information needed to score presence and severity of symptoms. The instrument is divided into modules such as mood disorders, anxiety disorders, psychotic disorders, disruptive-behavior disorders, and incorporates an introductory, less-structured interview and screening section. The interviewer can select which modules are appropriate for individual clients based on clinical judgment. There is also freedom to include the viewpoints of different sources of information such as the parent, the child, school personnel, or the client's medical record. The version used in this project was the instrument developed by Axelson, Birmaher, Zelazny, Kaufman, and Gill (2009).

STRUCTURED INTERVIEW FOR PSYCHOSIS-RISK SYNDROMES (SIPS; MCGLASHAN, WALSH, AND WOODS, 2010)

An important piece of the comprehensive evaluation provided to project youth age ten and older was the Structured Interview for Psychosis-risk Syndromes (SIPS), a tool that was developed at the Yale PRIME prodromal research clinic. This clinic operates in the same community mental-health center where one of the programs that we described in chapter 2, Specialized Treatment Early in Psychosis (STEP), is located. Our project staff was trained at Yale by one of the authors of the SIPS to reliably administer and score it.

SIPS aims to evaluate risk for developing a psychotic disorder (e.g., schizophrenia or schizoaffective disorder) by looking for advance signs of disturbance in functioning. The instrument allows providers to identify the possible presence of a prodromal phase of illness and intervene early, as opposed to only identifying the illness after a full psychotic break. The risk syndromes evaluated by SIPS include: attenuated positive symptom psychosis risk syndrome, brief intermittent psychotic symptom psychosis risk syndrome, and genetic risk and deterioration psychosis risk syndrome.

DEMOGRAPHIC CHARACTERISTICS OF THE YOUTH

Demographic characteristics of the final sample of youth enrolled in the project also are described here. Participating youth were ethnically diverse, between the ages of 8- and 19-years old and current recipients of mental-health services in selected agency day treatment, outpatient clinic, and residential programs in the Hudson Valley and New York City regions of New York State. In the charts, similarities and differences between the three groups of youth (project, screened, and agency) are shown regarding gender, age ranges, ethnicities, the program types in which youth receive care, and the diagnoses that they had at the time of screening.

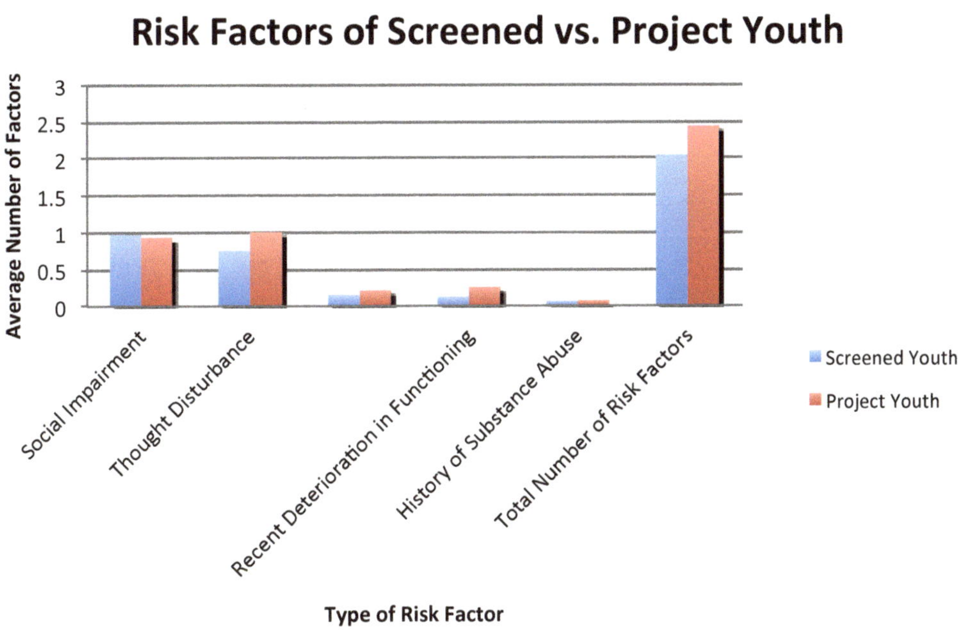

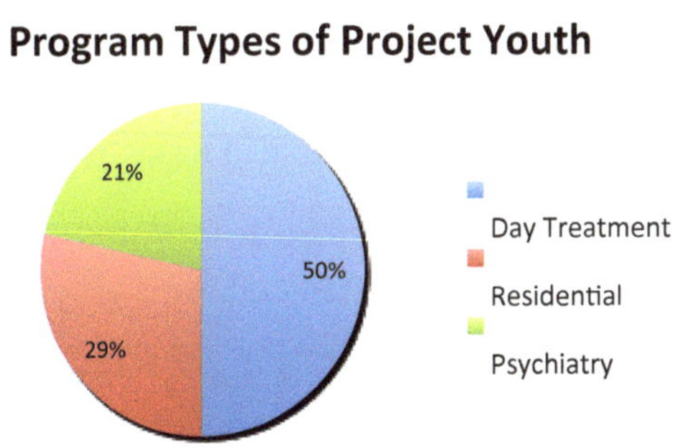

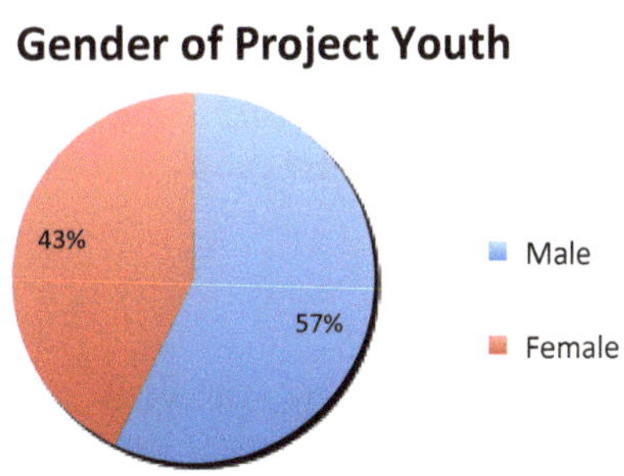

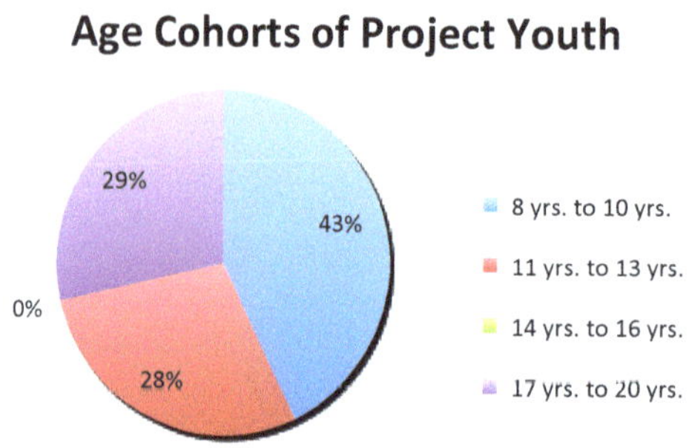

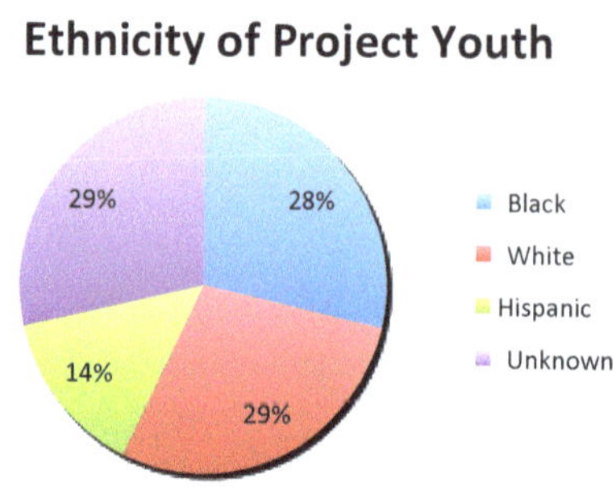

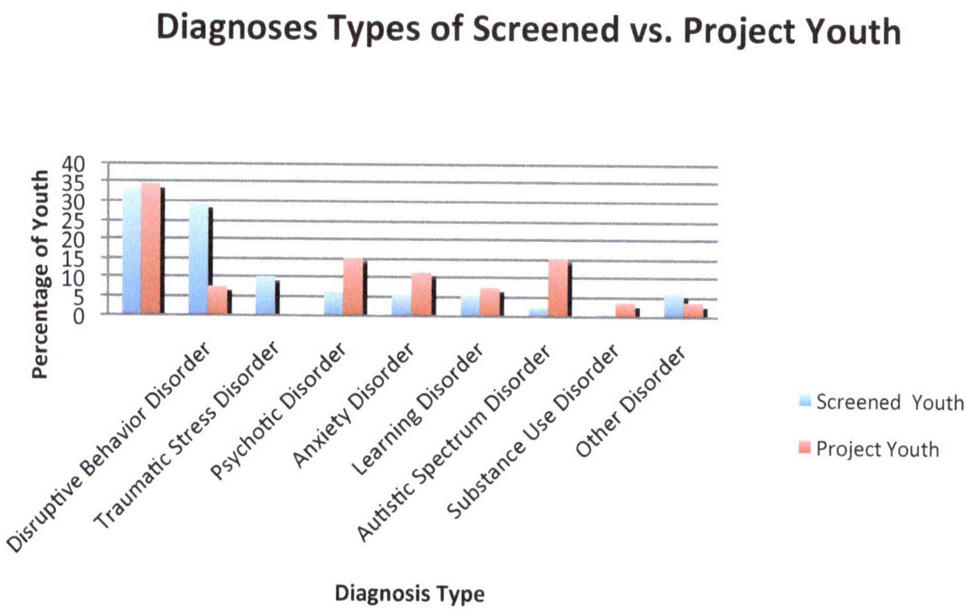

CASE EXAMPLE

In the interest of illustrating in detail the enhancement of care as usual that came with the project participation, here is an example of a youth and family's experience of the project from the time of enrollment through evaluation, consultation, and follow-up:

The family and researcher met to discuss the project and obtain informed consent, and were joined by the youth upon family approval. The youth was accompanied by his clinician at the day-treatment program he attends, and the clinician sat down with the researcher, family, and youth, to participate in a discussion about what would happen during the evaluation, the consultation, and afterward. Family and youth discussed how participation might be beneficial and agreed to proceed with the evaluation. The researcher met with the young man and his family, together and separately, depending on clinical judgment, over the course of the two-session evaluation.

During each session, the researcher got to know the youth and family, and asked structured questions to assist in diagnosis and evaluate psychosis risk. Questions covered a variety of topics: experiences, symptoms, strengths, and goals; multiple sources provided information. After the evaluation was complete, a meeting was scheduled for the consultation. The youth and family attended this meeting, which took place a few weeks after the evaluation was completed. It was a meeting wherein the young man recognized several different people in his life: his family, his therapist, the psychiatrist, and the evaluator. During the meeting the evaluator talked about what was learned during the evaluation, taking care to describe both needs and strengths, and presented a thorough understanding of the youth as a person and the areas in which he struggled. Next, the evaluator discussed recommendations—using a menu of best practices with evidence-based treatments for the youth's particular problems. Everyone in the room talked about the options for interventions and decided on a plan of care.

About a week later, a written version of the plan was developed during the meeting and was distributed to the family as well as to the treatment providers.

Then, his treatment providers and family started doing some of the things that had been planned. The researcher followed up with the family, youth, and treatment providers at one month, two months, four months, six months, nine months, and twelve months post-consultation to see how the youth was doing, how things were going with the plan, and what help was still needed. When the care providers asked for information and resources to implement the interventions recommended and planned, the research team provided what was needed to move the plan forward. Upon the completion of one year post-consultation, the researchers concluded follow-up contact with the family and encouraged them to seek out providers for any ongoing care coordination that was needed.

SUMMARY AND CONCLUSION

The project provided the opportunity to augment substantially care for youth that need it the most—youth at risk for psychotic episodes. Using a component of the standard initial-assessment procedures to screen youth for psychosis and risk of psychosis, we invited the identified youth and their families to participate not only in an enhanced assessment and consultation service, but also in specialized treatment protocols.

We encountered some barriers to implementing the project and implemented additional interventions to address emerging barriers. One most commonly cited was a lack of sufficient time (on the part of busy clinicians) to implement the identified intervention (e.g., above described discovery of the need for provider time to attend school meetings and to advocate). Examples of other barriers included the regional or local unavailability of an evidence-based, indicated intervention (e.g., social-skills group near the client's home or school) and youth deterioration in functioning early in enrollment (precluding delivery of the outpatient menu of interventions). Finally, sometimes clients or families decided later to discontinue recommended interventions for their own reasons.

As discussed above, the project youth received an enhanced service package including comprehensive evaluation, consultation in collaboration with families, evaluators, and care providers regarding best practices, and continued support to encourage implementation of evidence-based interventions and to overcome barriers. In one typical example, social-skills training was recommended for a particular youth in the project, and the youth's clinician realized during this discussion that she already had the professional training and materials to deliver this treatment method. She then decided to use the protocol to train social skills in the young person's classroom therapy group in standard day treatment programming. Ongoing feedback from and adjustment to the expressed needs of project participants and treatment providers allowed us to fine-tune this package, resulting in improved care for all participants.

CHAPTER FOUR

Collaborative, contextualized consultation and technical assistance: Recommended best practices

The consultation component of the project was a collaborative process that supported the use of evidence-based interventions. The youth, his or her primary caregivers, and his or her treatment team (e.g., primary clinician, psychiatrist, schoolteacher, case manager, and family advocate) were invited to attend and participate in the consultation and technical-assistance session, which typically took place one to four weeks after completion of the comprehensive evaluation. Throughout this chapter, each component of the consultation session is described step-by-step, with an emphasis on the recommended evidence-based and best practice interventions. The consultation session provided an opportunity for critical members involved in the youth's care to collaboratively review the comprehensive-evaluation findings and discuss possible interventions meant to enhance the youth's existing treatment plan.

Each consultation session began with a brief introduction and overview, during which the research psychologist explained the purpose of the session, reviewed the agenda, and emphasized collaborative goal setting, encouraging youth and caregivers to provide input and ask questions at any time. Each participant was given the consultation and technical-assistance packet, including the session agenda; the Best Practices Checklist of the project; Family Psycho-education, Social Skills Training, and Cognitive Skills Training worksheets; and any appropriate supplemental materials such as a nutrition and lifestyle-intervention literature review or a list of helpful Website links for families of youth struggling with mental illness.

After all session participants were familiar with the purpose and structure of the session, the research psychologist provided feedback from the comprehensive evaluation. The reason for referral to the project, the youth's presenting problems and diagnosis, and the young person and family's needs and strengths were reviewed. Again, participants were encouraged to ask questions and provide input throughout the session.

Considerable research indicates the benefit of early intervention for the treatment of psychotic illnesses via an assortment of evidence-based treatments, such as family psycho-education, social-skills training, cognitive remediation, supported employment or education services, and pharmacotherapy (Baksheev, Allott, Jackson, McGorry, and Killackey, 2012; Norman and Breitborde, 2014). A new model of treatment further incorporates a team-based therapeutic approach focused on recovery that emphasizes a seamless transition from adolescence to adulthood (Lieberman, Dixon, and Goldman, 2013). This information was used to inform the development of the Best Practices Checklist for outlining the recommended interventions. After providing session participants with this menu of possible interventions, discussion focused on the ways each intervention applied to the youth's unique circumstances. The interventions recommended were either evidence-based or best practices meant to enhance the youth's existing treatment plan and fell into one of the five following categories: family psycho-education, social-skills training, cognitive-skills training, care coordination, and psychiatry/medical interventions.

FAMILY PSYCHO-EDUCATION

Psychotic disorders often are characterized by early symptom manifestation, with the first episode occurring during youth or adolescence (Gearing, 2008). Because youth typically live with and depend on their families, the responsibility of managing and supporting conditions associated with psychotic disorders often falls on the family. Providing families with diagnostic information, support, coping skills, and problem-solving skills early on has been found to reduce the trauma of illness-onset and prevent development of dysfunctional family patterns, resulting in positive outcomes for youth and their families (Gearing, 2008; Lucksted, McFarlane, Downing, Dixon, and Adams, 2012).

Project family psycho-educational interventions involved helping family members understand the youth's diagnosis, implications of the diagnosis and the potential for recovery, and providing information about best practices, such as problem-solving training and strategies for coping. Family psycho-education began during the consultation session as the research psychologist provided information about the youth's diagnosis and related best practices, and the importance of consistency in treatment, wellness self-management, and family empowerment. Additionally, the research psychologist utilized the core components of family psycho-education throughout the entire consultation session; these components include joining (i.e., building a respectful, supportive relationship with the family that embraces individual and cultural differences); education (i.e., helping family members understand the youth's illness and available treatment options); problem-solving (i.e., working with the family to identify and understand the problem, collaboratively agree upon a solution, and make a specific plan to move forward); structural change in the treatment (i.e., working with the family to establish a respectful environment in which all members feel empowered to utilize their strengths); and multi-family contact (i.e., encouraging the family to participate in local family support groups).

SOCIAL-SKILLS TRAINING

Social-skills impairment is common in psychosis, especially early onset psychosis (Hollis, 2003). Social skills and social competence are viewed as protective factors that help individuals with psychosis stabilize their illness, improve adherence to treatment, promote progress toward recovery, and enhance their quality of life (Kopelowicz, Liberman, and Zarate, 2006). Social-skills training, an evidence-based practice that teaches individuals to communicate their emotions and needs effectively both verbally/orally and nonverbally, has been found to result in positive outcomes and improve certain aspects of social competence (Mueser, Deavers, Penn, and Cassisi, 2013).

Project social-skills training interventions involved teaching the youth how to appropriately communicate and interact with others, both verbally/orally and nonverbally, in order to enhance social competence and relate with others in a mutually reinforcing and reciprocal fashion. Recommended interventions falling under this category were sub-categorized as follows: general social-skills training (e.g., direct instruction, role play, feedback, and home assignments), individual social-skills training, group social-skills training, basic social-skills training, and complex social-skills training.

COGNITIVE-SKILLS TRAINING

Individuals with or at risk for psychosis often exhibit diminished cognitive abilities (e.g., attention, memory, executive functioning, social cognition, and metacognition) compared to those without psychosis (Piskulic, Barbato, Liu, and Addington, 2015). Cognitive deficits are related to poor functional outcomes and may be particularly disruptive during adolescence because this is a critical time for learning (Piskulic, Barbato, Lui, and Addington, 2015). Cognitive-remediation therapy has been found to improve cognition and functioning in adults with schizophrenia (Wykes, Huddy, Cellard, McGurk, and Czobor, 2011). Although only a few recent studies explore the effects of cognitive-skills training for specifically high-risk, younger populations, those that did, found moderate improvements in cognition and functioning (Piskulic, Barbato, Liu, and Addington, 2015).

Project cognitive-skills training interventions targeted improved cognitive processes, including attention, memory, executive function, social cognition, and metacognition. If deemed appropriate, youth were given the option to participate in C8 Sciences. C8 Sciences is an online brain-training program that utilizes progressive sequences of cognitive exercises similar to many computer games, aiming to restore cognitive capacities. C8 Sciences was designed by neuroscientist Bruce E. Wexler, MD, to strengthen the following eight core cognitive capacities: sustained attention, response inhibition, speed of information processing, cognitive flexibility and control, multiple simultaneous attention, working memory, category formation, and pattern recognition and inductive thinking. Depending on the youth's specific context, the C8 Sciences program is for home use or treatment program use. In some cases, other activities aimed to improve focus and executive functioning were recommended such as martial arts, yoga, or meditation.

CARE COORDINATION

Individuals with chronic illnesses such as psychosis often partake in a comprehensive array of services that requires continuity of care and extensive coordination across treatment providers to be successful (Anderson and Knickman, 2001). Unfortunately, the mental-health system is often fragmented, decentralized, and uncoordinated, resulting in discontinuity of care, disengagement from treatment, and increased risk for negative outcomes (Kreyenbuhl, Nossel, and Dixon, 2009).

"To correct" for this common experience in treatment, the project care-coordination interventions were individualized and varied, and designed to assist youth and their families with navigation of their complex systems of care. Specific care-coordination recommendations included sharing the final technical-assistance plan (i.e., the action plan developed during the consultation session) with other providers involved in the youth's treatment, providing a letter summarizing the evaluation results to other individuals or entities involved in the youth's care, and advocating for changes to the youth's educational plan. Other interventions in this category involved advocating for coordination between care systems, providing information about advocacy and peer-support groups, coordinating referral to specialized treatment services, and empowering caregivers to lead the care coordination effort. Throughout all care coordination interventions, strong emphasis was placed on the importance of consistency in treatment focus across treatment and educational settings.

PSYCHIATRY/MEDICAL INTERVENTIONS

Published trials using antipsychotic medications show evidence of reducing conversion to full-blown psychosis and improving current symptoms (Agius and Butler, 2012; Liu and Demjaha, 2013). Similarly, other medications and supplements including but not limited to antidepressants, omega-3 fatty acids, lithium, and antioxidants may prevent abnormal brain changes that take place during prodromal psychosis, resulting in improved functioning and delaying or preventing the onset of full-blown psychosis (Agius and Butler, 2012). Although past research has shown favorable outcomes, medications used to treat psychosis are often accompanied by adverse side effects, necessitating extreme precaution when prescribing (Liu and Demjaha, 2013). Medication management is an extremely individualized process that requires appropriate instructions, education, and monitoring (Liu and Demjaha, 2013).

Project psychiatry and medical interventions involved recommendations meant to ensure that the youth received appropriate medical, psychiatric, and medication-management services. When applicable, prescribers were advised to monitor for psychosis, consider changes in medications to target psychosis or mood dysregulation, and monitor or review medications with side effects in mind. If the treating psychiatrist was not present, arrangements were made to share the technical-assistance plan with the psychiatrist. Additionally, if a new diagnosis was made based on the comprehensive evaluation findings, a formal diagnosis change to the youth's treatment plan was recommended.

After discussion of the proposed recommended inter-ventions, consultation session participants were urged to share their feedback before creating a formal action plan. Strategies already in place to address the youth and family's needs were identified and the youth and family were asked to share their ideas about what was needed from services. The youth, family, and treatment providers identified interventions from "the menu" provided that they wanted to pursue, and a written action plan, i.e., the technical-assistance plan, was formulated. Each action step was explicitly linked to one member of the youth's team and a timeline associated with implementation identified. It is important to note that not all of the five intervention categories were recommended for every youth in the project. Only those interventions that were deemed appropriate for the youth's unique circumstances were recommended, and only those interventions that were collectively agreed upon during the consultation session were incorporated into the technical-assistance plan.

At the conclusion of the consultation session, the activities of the meeting were briefly summarized and the next steps regarding follow-up contact were discussed. Each individual present left the session with a clear understanding of expectations for the youth's future treatment; in the coming days, a typed version of the technical-assistance plan formulated by all present at the consultation session was either mailed or e-mailed to all that attended.

CHAPTER FIVE

Case study

In the following case study, all identifying information has been changed to protect the confidentiality of the youth and family, but the material presented accurately represents the fundamental elements of this youth's (whom we call Jessica) journey through the project.

Born in a Central American country, Jessica displayed maladaptive behavior early in life. At two-and-a-half, she was often described as "different." She was aggressive with other children in her preschool class without provocation, often played by herself rather than with her peers, and generally would not look directly into other people's eyes. Eventually, Jessica was diagnosed with autism.

Adding to Jessica's difficulties, as a young child she witnessed domestic violence between her parents, and was beaten by her father. Eventually, Jessica's mother moved to the United States. Jessica remained with her father for about two years, and then joined her mother in the U.S. when she was about nine-years old. Once in the States, Jessica attended an outpatient mental-health counseling center for a little under a year; eventually, her school district referred her to one of our agency day-treatment programs, citing a need for a therapeutic setting to improve her functioning in school. Jessica started at this day-treatment program at sixteen, and was diagnosed with Depressive Disorder Not Otherwise Specified and Pervasive Developmental Disorder Not Otherwise Specified in this setting. In the coming years, Jessica was repeatedly hospitalized for aggression, violence, and suicidal ideation.

In Jessica's nineteenth year, clinical staff at her program referred her for participation in the AMHF Early Intervention for Psychosis Project. As a result of this referral, project staff conducted a comprehensive chart review of Jessica's care to date to determine if she did present with variables predictive of psychosis risk. At the time of her chart review, Jessica was having a great deal of trouble with aggression and anxiety about what she thought was "wrong with her." Her peer relations were difficult and she was often teased and bullied. She also was exhibiting unusual thought content including paranoid ideation. Jessica's clinician, Maureen, suspected a more severe diagnosis than her current diagnoses of Mood Disorder Not Otherwise Specified, Obsessive-compulsive Disorder, and Asperger's Disorder. By this time, Jessica had been diagnosed with many different disorders at different times, including Pervasive Developmental Disorder, Attention-Deficit/Hyperactivity Disorder, Oppositional Defiant Disorder, and Depressive Disorder Not Otherwise Specified. The inconsistency of her diagnosis among providers over time made Jessica an ideal candidate for the project.

When Jessica's chart review was completed, three psychosis-risk factors were evident: thought disturbance, social impairment, and genetic risk due to a maternal aunt with a possible diagnosis of Psychotic Disorder Not Otherwise Specified. Maureen reached out to Jessica and her family, gave them a general introduction to the project, and let them know someone else would be in contact to describe the project further. The research psychologist called Jessica's mother, Adelaide, shortly thereafter, and explained the project in more detail. Adelaide thought the project might benefit her daughter, and together they scheduled a time for the first of two comprehensive-evaluation meetings.

At the time of her comprehensive evaluation, Jessica was diagnosed by her treatment team with Mood Disorder Not Otherwise Specified, Obsessive-compulsive Disorder, Asperger's Disorder, and had a rule-out diagnosis of Bipolar Disorder. Over the course of two, two-hour meetings, the research psychologist and another project-staff member met with Jessica, Adelaide, and Maureen individually and in combination. First, the research team obtained informed consent from Jessica and her mother. Then, three separate assessment tools were administered in order to evaluate Jessica's current status: the Kiddie-Schedule for Affective Disorders and Schizophrenia (Axelson, Birmaher, Zelazny, Kaufman, and Gill, 2009); the Structured Interview for Psychosis-Risk (McGlashan, Walsh, and Woods, 2010); and the Child and Adolescent Needs and Strengths—NY assessment (Lyons, 2011). Findings suggested that Jessica met diagnostic criteria for Autism Spectrum Disorder and

Mood Disorder Not Otherwise Specified, but that no psychotic disorder or psychosis-risk syndrome was present. These findings suggested that Jessica was not in the proper treatment setting, but required services that would address her developmental disabilities more directly. It was suspected that many of Jessica's struggles over the years were due, in part, to a lack of support for her developmental disability-related needs.

When the research psychologist contacted Adelaide to confirm the date of a meeting to review evaluation findings and provide consultation about treatment, the research team learned that Jessica had been rehospitalized due to physical aggression against her mother and the verbalization of suicidal thoughts. Adelaide was overwhelmed, and thought the consultation should be postponed. The research team contacted Maureen to follow-up, and Maureen said she had been working very closely with Adelaide since Jessica's most recent hospitalization. Maureen thought that the consultation meeting might be helpful toward calming Adelaide's anxiety about her daughter and help her explore options for Jessica's care. Maureen also thought the consultation meeting would be an opportunity to develop a plan to help Jessica function optimally in the community, which, with her current hospitalization status, was of utmost importance. Maureen then spoke with Adelaide, and Adelaide agreed that proceeding with the consultation as planned would be a good idea.

Three members of the research team—Maureen, Jessica's psychiatrist, and Adelaide—attended the consultation meeting. At many consultations in the project, the youth was also invited to be present, depending on his or her level of functioning.

Unfortunately, Jessica was still in the hospital and was unable to attend.

Adelaide appeared to be overwhelmed and stressed during the consultation. As a result, the research team suggested several interventions but focused on supporting and empowering Adelaide and exploring what she believed would be most helpful for her daughter. Adelaide appeared to respond well to this support. She expressed enthusiasm for the offer to help coordinate and secure proper care for Jessica, as she was concerned about Jessica and her family's safety once Jessica was discharged from the hospital.

After evaluation results were reviewed, the following evidence-based interventions were suggested (wording taken directly from the written action plan):

Family Psycho-education: (1) Treatment providers will work with Jessica and Adelaide on Wellness Self-management Skills (especially Independent Living skills and Illness Management skills). This will include direct instruction and repeated practice of specific skills, structured so that all providers are working with Jessica on the same skill at the same time.

Social Skills: (1) Treatment providers will train social skills in group and individual therapy by breaking specific skills down into component parts and using live rehearsal, feedback, and family homework assignments to practice these skills. (2) Jessica should be placed in vocational settings with a low level of social challenge until she has made enough progress to function successfully in a more challenging setting.

Care Coordination: (1) The research team will contact Jessica's Medicaid Services Coordinator (MSC) at a neighboring agency to advocate for placement in New York State's Office for People with Developmental Disabilities (OPWDD) short-term crisis housing if she is discharged from the hospital before the school year begins (i.e., before she would be receiving care through her current setting, which operated via the academic calendar). (2) With the support of Maureen, Adelaide will call an emergency Committee on Special Education (CSE) meeting to begin coordinating a transition to receive services within a care system that can simultaneously address her multiple, complex developmental needs and her psychiatric needs. (3) The research team will write a letter summarizing the results of Jessica's evaluation to provide to those at the CSE meeting to support the process of transitioning between care systems.

Psychiatric/Medical: (1) Jessica's psychiatrist will review her medications and continue to monitor Jessica for risk for psychosis.

All interventions were agreed upon by those present at the consultation meeting, and the research team offered continued support for Adelaide, Jessica, and Jessica's treatment team in any way that they could. As demonstrated by the prevalence of care-coordination interventions suggested via the technical-assistance model, a tremendous part of working toward Jessica's improvement would involve care coordination.

In the days following the consultation meeting, the research team worked with Jessica's family and Maureen, as well as

Jessica's MSC, to schedule a meeting at the state office to discuss Jessica's needs and attempt to secure further supports. With prompting from the research team, the MSC made a referral to the state office for both respite services immediately following Jessica's hospital discharge to help provide Adelaide with some reprieve (i.e., 30 days' overnight stay in a facility designed to meet Jessica's needs), and in the long-term, residential services for Jessica that would address her complex developmental and psychiatric needs. This meeting with the state aimed to determine if Jessica was truly eligible for these services, and to determine the urgency of these issues. As indicated in the technical-assistance plan, the research psychologist wrote a letter outlining findings of the comprehensive evaluation and their recommendations, helping to demonstrate that Jessica truly was eligible for enhanced services and services that addressed her developmental disabilities, and furthermore that her need was indeed urgent. The research team helped facilitate a plan for two members of the team to attend the meeting with this letter, along with Maureen and Adelaide, to advocate for Jessica's care.

In the meantime, the research team worked to support Jessica's family in other ways. They helped facilitate Maureen's discussions with Adelaide and Jessica about Jessica's transition home from the hospital, and that Jessica's psychiatrist would make sure Jessica had an as-needed medication prescribed to help ease this transition home.

Unfortunately, the meeting with the state office was canceled since the official said that the kind of referral made for Jessica should be handled through the school district. Because of this,

Maureen, Adelaide, and the research team altered their tactics toward using the emergency CSE meeting, already in the process of being set up because of the second care-coordination intervention suggested at the consultation meeting, as a forum in which to coordinate proper care for Jessica.

The research psychologist accompanied Adelaide to the CSE meeting about a month after the consultation, and with them brought the letter summarizing evaluation results and subsequent recommendations in order to advocate for Jessica's appropriate residential placement. Unfortunately, at the time of the meeting Jessica was once again in the hospital. Adelaide, school representatives, the school principal of Jessica's day-treatment program, and Jessica's MSC attended this meeting. At the meeting, it was decided that the school district would seek an appropriate residential-school placement for Jessica; Adelaide consented to submit applications for several programs of this type. It also was determined that Jessica would remain in the agency's Day Treatment program in the event that she was discharged from the hospital before being placed in a residential setting. There was also some discussion of obtaining respite services for Adelaide and Jessica, in the event that Jessica was discharged from the hospital before the new school year began for the day-treatment program, as the CSE meeting was held during the summer while school was not in session.

In the coming weeks, just before the Labor Day weekend, Jessica was discharged from the hospital, where she had been since before the CSE meeting, and started school at her day-treatment program in early September. At this time, with the added support from the day-treatment program, Jessica was stable enough that respite services were not needed, and hospitalization was not required. Finally, a little over a month later, Jessica was admitted to a specialized autistic-spectrum unit in a residential-treatment program. When admission time came, Adelaide was nervous about leaving Jessica, until another girl from Jessica's assigned unit came up and welcomed her, calming many of both Jessica and Adelaide's fears.

As a part of the project, families were contacted at scheduled intervals over a twelve-month period to enquire about how the youth involved in the project was doing, and about the progress of the recommended and agreed-upon interventions planned at the consultation. The first two of these follow-ups occurred while the care-coordination activities previously described were taking place.

At the time of the first follow-up in early September, Jessica had just been discharged from the hospital and was home. By Adelaide's report, Jessica's behavior had stabilized and she was managing adequately at home. Adelaide thought that probably some of the medications that were prescribed during her most recent hospitalization played a role in this positive outcome. Because Jessica had just been released from the hospital, most of the interventions other than the care-coordination interventions were not applicable, as there had not been any time with Jessica out of the hospital to execute them (although the psychiatric/medical intervention was occurring, as Jessica's psychiatrist at her day-treatment program was monitoring her for psychosis, and keeping her on the same medications she had been prescribed while in the hospital, as those appeared to be working well for her). The care-coordination interventions had all been completed, and Adelaide was simply awaiting a placement within an appropriate residential program.

At the time of the second follow-up, Jessica had just been placed in her new residential program. Because she had recently changed care providers, most of the interventions recommended had not yet been implemented, as Jessica had not been at her new program long enough to implement a treatment plan fully. However, Jessica's functioning was improving—her problem behaviors identified during the Comprehensive Evaluation phase of the project were much better. Among other improvements, she was no longer having thoughts of hurting others.

At the remaining four follow-ups taking place over the next ten months, the research team spoke with Jessica's individual therapist at her residential placement, as well as Adelaide. All of Jessica's suggested interventions, excluding those that had previously been completed, were under way and going well at all follow-ups. In fact, the remaining recommended interventions that had not already been completed, such as working on Jessica's independent living skills, working on social skills by breaking them down into component parts, and being placed in a vocational setting with an appropriate level of social challenge, were all part of care as usual at her residential placement. Over the course of these follow-ups, Jessica's functioning across all areas (home, school, and work) was either the same or better from one time to the next. It is important to note that Jessica arrived at this placement, a placement that inherently met many of her needs, largely facilitated by the care-coordination interventions of the project, highlighting the key to the effectiveness of the comprehensive evaluation and technical assistance model.

At the final twelve-month follow-up, the research team thanked Jessica and Adelaide for their participation in the project, and asked them for any feedback that they might have. Adelaide expressed that she was pleased with the project, thought that it was helpful, and did not have anything that she would change about the experience of being involved with the project. The research team spoke with Jessica as well, who said she was doing pretty well, and enjoying her jobs at her residential-treatment setting. The research team reminded Jessica and Adelaide about the present monograph they were going to publish describing the project and its results, which they had originally been informed about during initial informed-consent procedures. The team asked Jessica and Adelaide if they would be open to having a chapter focus on their story to help exemplify the project, and to provide hope to others, viz., that individuals experiencing difficulties like Jessica's can significantly improve. Jessica and Adelaide both agreed that this would not be a problem, and consented to sharing their story.

This case powerfully elucidates the value of receiving focused-care coordination and support targeted to individual needs. As was suspected after the comprehensive-evaluation phase of the project, once Jessica was in the appropriate care setting that addressed both her psychiatric and her developmental needs, the improvement she demonstrated was dramatic. Jessica struggled with significant issues—auditory hallucinations, violent thoughts and actions, and extreme anxiety. The comprehensive evaluation made clear that she was not in the appropriate care setting, and through the technical-assistance model the research team was key in facilitating the switch for Jessica to a treatment setting more appropriate for her needs. Once in the proper setting, Jessica improved tremendously, in all likelihood largely due to the fact that almost all of the other interventions suggested at the consultation meeting were an integral part of that treatment setting.

CHAPTER SIX

The follow-up stage: Evaluation of youth functional outcomes and progress made on interventions planned

DISCUSSION OF FUNCTIONAL OUTCOMES FOR PROJECT YOUTH

Many areas of functioning were covered during follow-up contacts with families after the consultation session took place. A snapshot of the project youth functioning in the following areas provided a view into the potential impact of AMHF project participation: behavior in school; social functioning in school; behavior at home; need for supervision at home; risky behavior at home; relationship with caregiver; changes in problem behaviors identified during the evaluation; overall social impairment; and overall functioning. At each follow-up contact, families were asked to give examples of how youth were doing in each area, and encouraged to comment on the specific ways in which the youth appeared to have improved, gotten worse, or stayed the same since the previous contact. Therapists were also contacted and asked about youth functioning and what interventions were occurring; medical records were reviewed as part of follow-up data collection.

See the accompanying chart for a summary of functional change in the dozen project youth who completed follow up over one year (the "Case 11" youth dropped out of follow up prematurely and thus full data are not reported here).

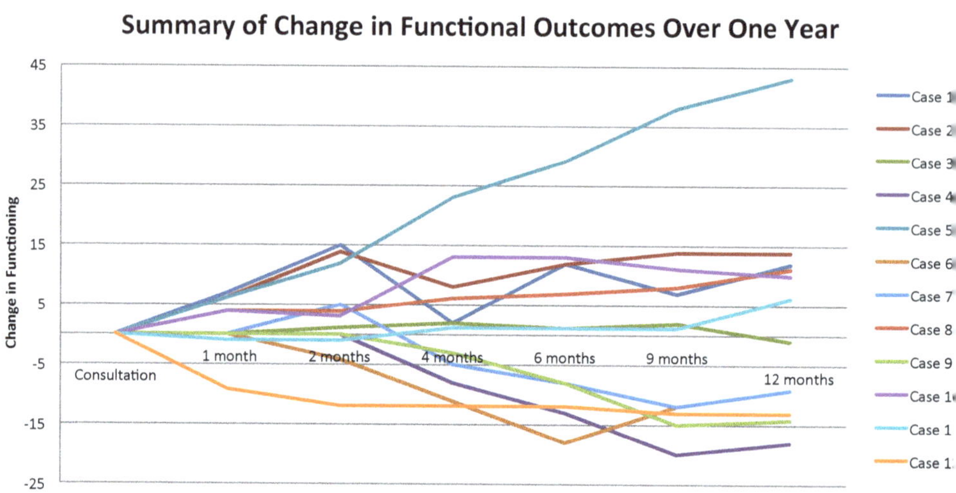

Mixed patterns of change in functioning over follow-up period were evident in the group of participants. Most of the young people studied exhibited some initial improvement followed by a pattern of alternating deterioration and improvement with a slightly positive trend. Five of the youth, however, exhibited a pattern of marked improvement across follow-up. Those five youth were examined separately, and the positive functional change they exhibited can be seen in the chart below:

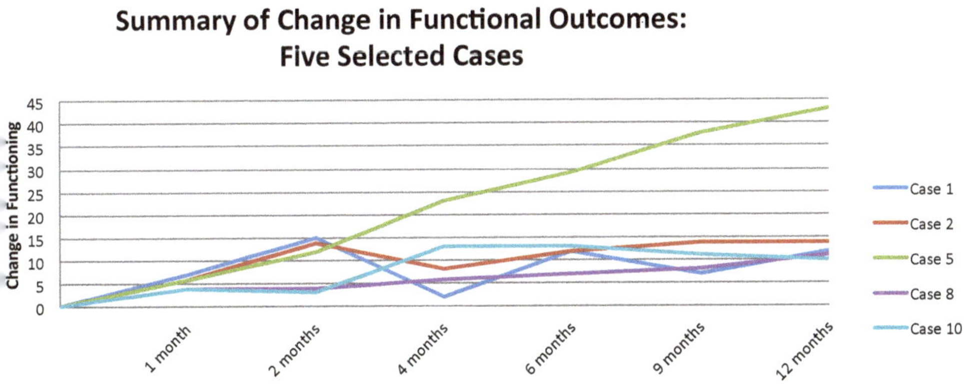

Three of these five project youth—Cases 2, 8, and 10—show a pattern of gradual improvement and maintenance of this level of functioning over time. Another project youth, Case 1, appears to have rapidly improved over the first two months post-consultation, but then rapidly deteriorated by four months' post-consultation, improved again at six months post-consultation, slightly deteriorated at nine-months post-consultation, and then made improvement at the one year mark. Moreover, a third project youth, Case 5, demonstrated significant, continuously improving functioning over the twelve months since consultation; more detailed information about this youth's progress is found in the preceding chapter 5, which provides a narrative description of the case study. Although they evinced different trajectories to improvement, at twelve-months post-consultation all five of these youth were functioning better than they were at the start of the project. The very different patterns of functional change in these five project youth necessitate a more detailed look at what changes took place. See the chart below for discrepancies between different areas of functional change regarding Case 1.

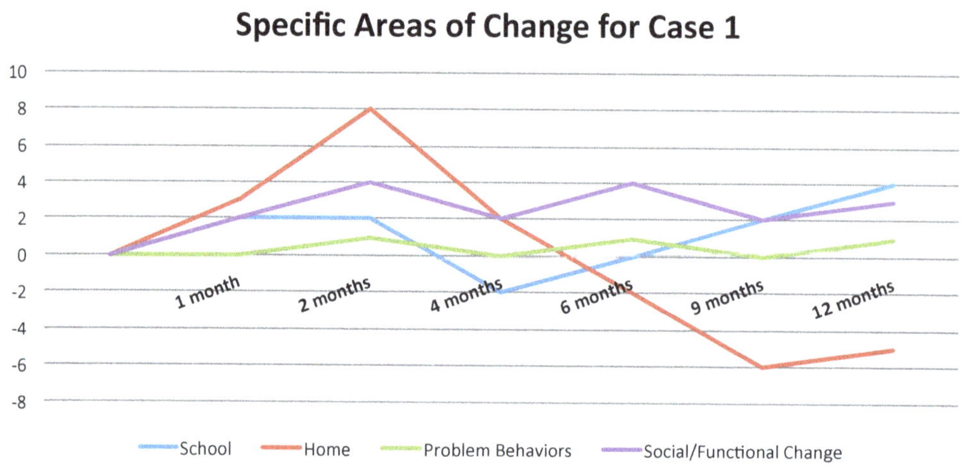

There are often ups and downs along the path of recovery for youth with significant behavioral health needs, and the case here shows this tendency. During the first two months post-consultation, gradual improvement in functional outcomes was reported at home and in school, with problems identified during the evaluation and in overall functioning. However, at the four-month follow-up the individual experienced deterioration in functioning both at home and at school. To understand this deterioration, the four-month follow-up occurred about one week after the start of the new school year—this is a stressful time for many families, particuarly for youth struggling with severe emotional and behavioral concerns. However, problem behaviors identified during the evaluation and overall functioning showed a more gradual deterioration than did functioning at home and at school at the four-month follow-up.

Between the four-month and six-month follow-ups, interventions for this youth were adjusted for these stressful times; specifically, the youth's educational plan was modified to resemble more closely the recommendation made during the consultation. Functioning at school then started on a trajectory of improvement, but it is clear from the graph that changes made at school were not associated with improvements at home. In fact, it was around this time that the youth was discharged from the in-home therapy services that had been in place when the family enrolled in the AMHF project. Without these supports in the home, the youth's functioning in that setting deteriorated. It is important to consider the significant challenges inherent in coordinating care among different settings in which the youth functions (i.e., school, home, therapy). Care coordination with those providing educational services for youth is an area of the intervention that is a key ingredient in early intervention for these youth.

Three youth participating in the project actually declined over the one-year post-consultation. These youth struggled even to maintain their baseline level of functioning, despite attempts made by the families and treatment providers to incorporate the recommended best practices into the youths' care plans. Barriers were clearly evident in implementing enhanced care plans for all twelve project youth, but certain youth clearly struggled. In these cases, depicted in the following graph, a schizophrenia-spectrum diagnosis had already been made either by the treatment team before the project started or by the research psychologist who conducted the comprehensive evaluation with the youth as part of the project. These findings support scientific studies that suggest premorbid intervention with youth at risk for psychosis is critical to a positive functional trajectory.

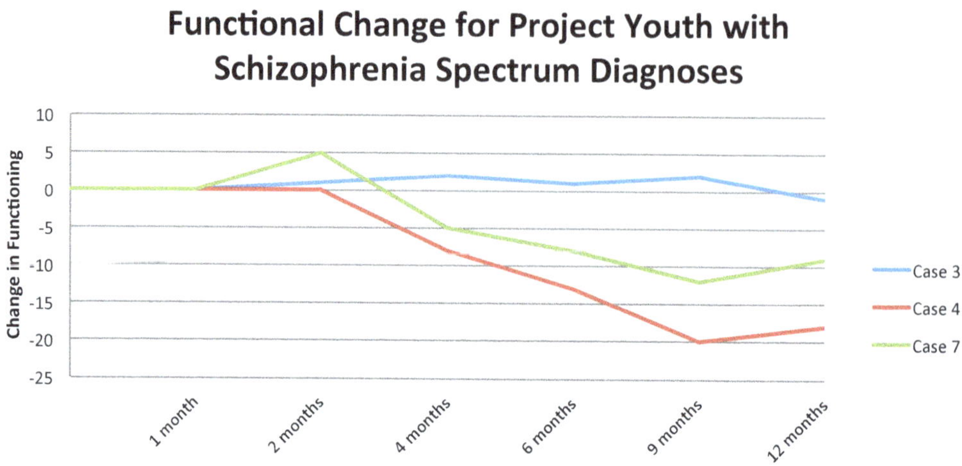

QUANTITATIVE ANALYSIS OF CANS-NY

Youth and family strengths and needs were assessed at three times in this project—during the comprehensive evaluation, six-months post-consultation, and at the one-year mark. We calculated the percentage of participants who demonstrated a sufficient level of change over the follow-up year using a statistical procedure known as the Reliable Change Index (RCI). The statistic allows a conclusion to be made about whether the amount of change observed in an individual case is enough to be categorized as real and meaningful. On all of the CANS-NY domains, we found that at least 91.67 percent of twelve youth were able to either maintain or improve their level of functioning or strength. In some areas however, Life Domain Functioning and Risk Behaviors, we saw that 8.33 percent (one youth) actually showed deterioration in functioning. We also assessed the youth's caregivers for strengths and needs, and found that all either maintained or gained strengths during the follow-up year. The full results are shown in the table.

PERCENTAGE OF PROJECT YOUTH WITH RELIABLE CHANGE IN STRENGTHS AND FUNCTIONING

CANS-NY Domain	Improved	Worsened	Maintained
Life Domain Functioning	16.67%	8.33%	75.00%
Risk Behaviors	33.33%	8.33%	58.33%
Behavioral Health Needs	33.33%	0.00%	66.67%
Youth Strengths	33.33%	0.00%	66.67%
Caregiver Strengths	16.67%	0.00%	83.33%
Caregiver Needs	0.00%	0.00%	100.00%

THE INTERVENTION TYPES

We wanted to learn more about which types of interventions the key people directing and implementing care for youth elected to pursue among the menu of best practices recommended in the consultation. To answer this question, we calculated the percentage of instances that the different types of interventions were chosen by the family and treatment providers. (See appendix A for a description of intervention types and subtypes. See appendix B for charts showing the frequency of care coordination and family psycho-education subtypes.)

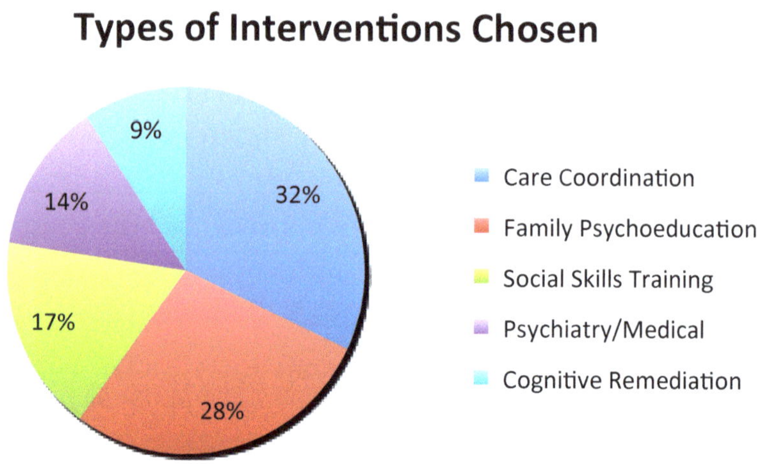

It is evident that family psychoeducation and care coordination were most frequently integrated into the care plan developed during the consultation. These two areas were important components of the enhancement of care being studied in this project. They also were the most complex of the intervention types since the actual tasks were highly individualized for each youth.

BARRIERS TO IMPLEMENTING BEST PRACTICES

During the follow-up stage of a youth's participation, we tried to learn about what might impede implementation of a recommended intervention. This information was a key component in understanding the impact of project participation on youth at risk for psychosis, and in addressing the gap commonly observed between what is considered best practice and what care is like in real-world treatment settings under less-than-ideal circumstances. We gathered information about these barriers, and found that the reasons given for not carrying out an intervention could be categorized as in the bar chart below.

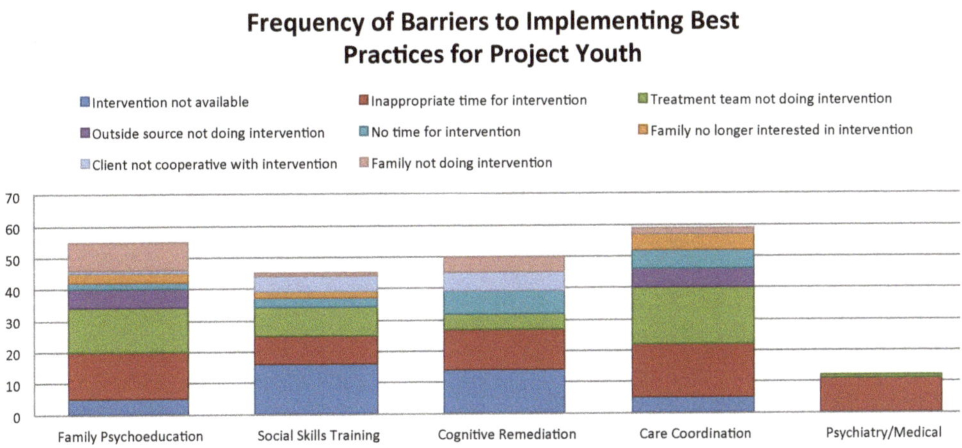

Most frequently, barriers to evidence-based interventions cited were lack of sufficient time on the part of overburdened providers and the lack of availability of a planned intervention. More numerous barriers were evident to providing family psychoeducation and care coordination. This finding is not surprising, given that psychoeducation and care coordination were the most complex and highly individualized of the intervention types recommended for youth in the project. On the other hand, psychiatry/medical interventions were more straightforward to carry out, and typically involved the continuation of interventions already being delivered. The system of "care as usual" did not have to change drastically, and few barriers were cited for this category of interventions.

For many youth in this project, social-skills training was identified as a recommended intervention and chosen by the youth, family, and team. However, barriers to implementation were apparent for all youth, and it was difficult for staff to provide adequate support and advocacy to overcome those barriers. The pie chart shows the frequency of barriers to social-skills training implementation that was evident across the one-year follow ups:

Barriers to Implementing Social Skills Training for Project Youth

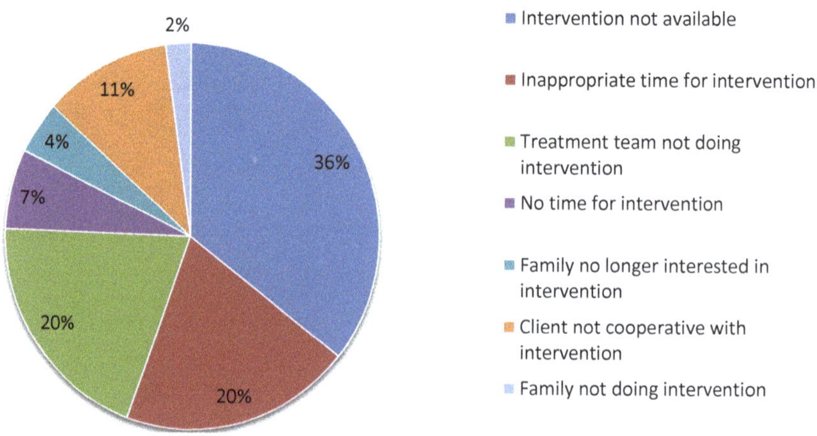

As shown, when social-skills training was recommended for a youth, 36 percent of the barriers families encountered were categorized as "Intervention not available." Social-skills training, despite its strong standing in the evidence base, was not easily accessed by families in their communities; and although the youth's treatment teams made attempts to initiate these interventions, they often reported a need to prioritize other activities that addressed more immediate clinical needs (seen in the pie chart: "Treatment team not doing intervention" at 20 percent and "Inappropriate time for intervention" at 20 percent).

Barriers to implementing planned evidence-based inter-ventions were evident in the case of a particular project youth who struggled to function well at school and at home. The school needed to cooperate with the family as well as with treatment providers to modify the care plan to address the psychiatric and educational needs identified during the evaluation. However, the family encountered significant challenges in the navigation of multiple systems through which the youth received services. Different parties had differing opinions on what level of care the youth needed, and there was no central point of coordination between the parties to facilitate the referrals that all needed to agree upon and put in place. In response, the research team played this role, and the resulting collaboration among the family, researchers, and treatment providers helped the youth access appropriate interventions that would have otherwise not been available. As is clear in the chart showing functional change for five project youth, this youth (Case 5) made demonstrable improvements in overall functioning. Follow up contact with the treatment providers and family indicated that the intervention was successful, and the family benefited from a combination of support and empowerment that was a direct result of the intervention and services offered through the AMHF project. The youth's care providers followed the recommendations made during the consultation regarding modifications and skill-building to take place in the home, school, and treatment settings. A focus of follow-up contact between the research team and the youth's caregiver was on empowering communication with providers about appropriately challenging the youth to build even more skills considering the great progress showed.

FAMILY FEEDBACK ON THE PROJECT

As part of the final follow-up contact with families, our staff asked for feedback enquiring specifically about what they found most helpful about their involvement in the project. Families reported that receiving diagnostic clarification and information about evidence-based treatments were positively experienced, in addition to the collaborative stance of the AMHF project with caregivers and clinicians to help navigate the complex systems of care serving these youth. For example, one of the care-coordination activities in highest demand was for project staff to advocate with the committees of professionals tasked with making decisions about appropriate services and placements for youth considering the diagnoses of serious psychiatric illness. In addition, several families described the regularly scheduled and structured follow-up calls to be helpful in themselves, stating that being asked the same questions about how their child was functioning in different areas and how that functioning compared to past levels of functioning was helpful because they could reflect on how far the youth had come, and understand the progress made over time instead of getting caught up in whatever issue was most pressing at the moment. This opportunity to step back and think about how care was helping or not helping allowed, according to families in this project, caregivers to better understand their child's needs based on both severities of illness and normal developmental changes, and to manage and support effective care.

CHAPTER SEVEN

Implications for treatment planning and program development: Implications of *The American Mental Health Foundation Early Intervention for Psychosis Project*

We conclude with an overview of what we learned from conducting this **AMHF Early Intervention for Psychosis Project** regarding implications for program development and improvement. In this project, we piloted an early intervention for psychosis service designed to provide palliative care and prevention for some of the most vulnerable and underserved individuals, viz., youth at risk for psychotic disorders. As part of this discussion, we present the necessity for flexible care management and advocacy for families involved in the multiple complex youth-serving systems that address treatment, legal, developmental, medical, and educational needs of young people who are experiencing severe mental illness. In addition, there is the importance of empowering families and youth to collaborate with service providers, asking for effective interventions based both on the evidence we have about best practices and the unique knowledge and expertise that *they* have about what works for them. The need for more comprehensive diagnostic assessment procedures in real-world practice settings and technical assistance and feedback along with ongoing care coordination is promoted here.

During the project, a snapshot of the youths' functioning at school and at home provided a view into the potential impact of project participation. We examined varying trajectories seen in youth and conducted a quantitative analysis of a measure of youth and family needs as well as strengths as assessed at three time points: during the comprehensive evaluation, six months post-consultation, and at the one-year mark. We charted individual youth progress and statistically measured change with the Reliable Change Index, allowing us to interpret each individual's progress as shown through the charts in the preceding chapter. Findings demonstrate that youth at risk for psychosis typically experience peaks and valleys in functioning; but that it is possible, before youth are fully converted to a psychotic disturbance, to facilitate improved outcomes—and even gains in strengths—with focused and collaboratively planned, effective treatment.

In this study, we learned a great deal about what elements of our protocol were helpful to youth, and what evidence-based elements provided markedly difficult-to-implement in real-world-care settings wherein services are provided. Social-skills training, care coordination, and advocacy were needed, impactful when provided, but most difficult to implement with youth in our service-delivery system.

The absence of available social-skills training, and the difficulties we encountered in encouraging providers to implement that training, were particularly concerning. Social-skills training has ample support in the evidence base for many challenged youth, and youth at risk for psychosis or experiencing psychosis can benefit considerably from social training. To maximize effectiveness, a group facilitator must provide direct instructions on specific skills, facilitate modeling or role-play rehearsal of the skills, and give youth positive corrective feedback on their actual behavior. There were few, if any, social skills with these characteristics available to youth in the AMHF–Astor project due to the dearth of adequately trained clinicians to facilitate them.

The significant level of administrative and case load burden apparent in the work lives of providers further complicated matters. Even though some providers were motivated (once educated about the potential benefit of social-skills training) to provide such groups, they cited insufficient time to learn and implement a new intervention as a significant barrier to their own success.

Time barriers are also evident in our attempts to encourage advocacy and care coordination from providers. Throughout the project, our research team addressed these barriers by providing limited case-management support to families ourselves, and we found that families in need of resources to help overcome systems' barriers were able to benefit from this support. For example, to assist the treatment teams and families in finding social-skills training for youth, we offered to compile lists of social-skills training groups in the community and gave information about specific skills-training protocols that clinicians could use. There were also times when advocacy for care coordination between a youth's educational and mental-health care was needed, and in these cases there were times when the research psychologist attended meetings to support the youth or wrote a letter documenting the diagnostic findings and recommendations from the comprehensive evaluation. Our experiences mirror the extensive support for care coordination and advocacy in the literature, and the absence of these services in the overall agency-care system is concerning.

Of note is the fact that, at the time of this writing (spring 2015), previously limited care-coordination services are being expanded in mental health as a key element of Medicaid health-care reform. Our findings support the importance of this change.

As part of the final follow-up contact with families, we asked for their feedback enquiring specifically about what they found most helpful about their involvement in the project. Families reported that receiving information about diagnosis and evidence-based treatments were positively experienced, in addition to the collaborative stance of the project with caregivers and clinicians to help navigate the complex systems of care serving these youth. Repeatedly, research in health and behavioral health care has supported the effectiveness of a collaborative, feedback-seeking stance with patients (see, for example, Norcross and Wampold, 2011). However, clinical providers frequently perceive routine collaborative assessment of treatment effectiveness throughout care as burdensome to families:

a waste of time in the context of treatment contacts (Garland, Kruse, and Aarons, 2003).

Family participants in this project support that research with their report that regular follow-up, involving a review of their youth's progress and current needs and strengths, was actually considered a helpful *intervention.* Measurement of outcomes can (and in our case *was)* perceived positively by service recipients and should be explicitly incorporated into care provision.

Providers of "care as usual" to youth at risk for psychotic disturbance might use our experience to target changes in service-delivery systems. Priorities for increasing successful care for these struggling youth include increasing access to full, fine-tuned diagnostic procedures with functional assessment as a key component, and providing critically needed social-skills training, advocacy, and care coordination by managing clinician caseloads and providing adequate training and supervision. In addition, educating and empowering caregivers, providing the advocacy and support that the *caregivers* value and require, and assessing progress collaboratively throughout course of treatment can heighten care effectiveness considerably. Finally, ongoing measurement of functional outcomes that leads to active changes in treatment planning and delivery was found in the AMHF–Astor project to be a key element of treatment success.

Appendix A
Menu of interventions

Menu of Interventions Offered to AMHF Youth	
Intervention	*Subtypes*
Family Psychoeducation	Provide information to family about diagnosis
	Provide information to youth about diagnosis
	Provide information about evidence based treatment
	Provide information about typical child/adolescent development
	Educate treatment team/family about need for consistency in approach
	Provide information about wellness self-management/family empowerment resources
Social Skills Training	General social skills training
	Individual social skills training
	Group social skills training
	Focus on basic social skills
	Focus on more complex social skills
Cognitive Skills Training	C8 Sciences at home
	C8 Sciences at treatment program
	Other activities to improve focus and executive functioning
Care Coordination	Share Technical Assistance plan with other providers
	Letter summarizing evaluation results
	Advocate for changes to educational plan
	Advocate for coordination between care systems
	Provide information about advocacy and peer support groups
	Help coordinate case management/care coordination services
	Help coordinate referral to specialized treatment services
	Empower family to lead coordination efforts
Psychiatric/Medical	Monitor for psychosis
	Consider change in medications to target psychosis
	Consider change in medications to target mood dysregulation
	Share Technical Assistance plan with treating psychiatrist because they were not at consultation meeting
	Monitor/review medications with side effects in mind

APPENDIX B

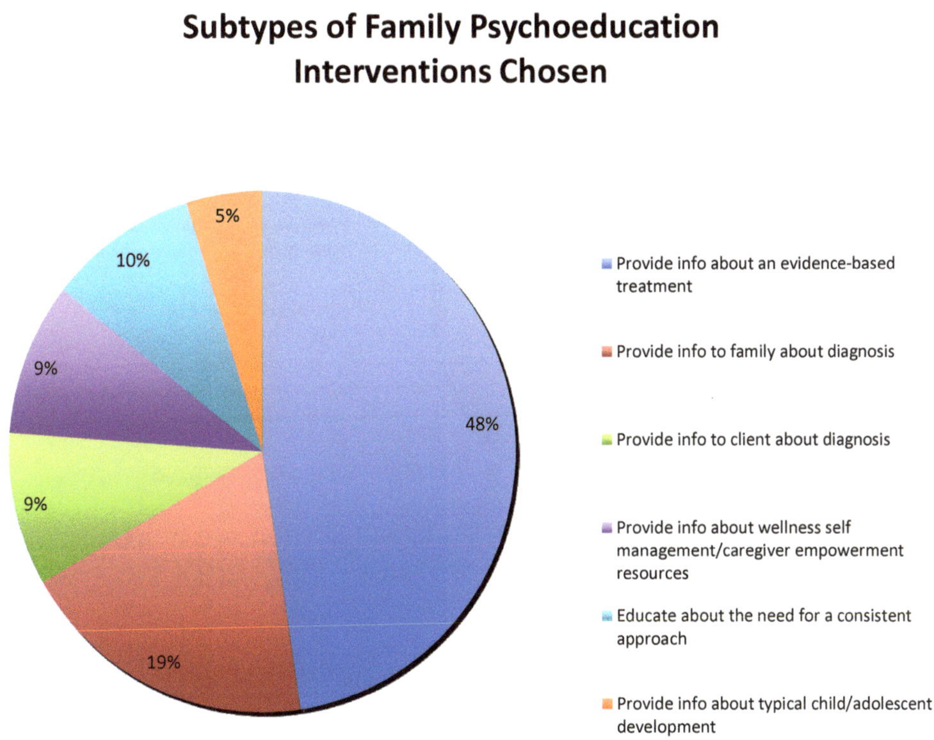
Subtypes of Family Psychoeducation Interventions Chosen
5%
10%
9%
9%
19%
48%
Provide info about an evidence-based treatment
Provide info to family about diagnosis
Provide info to client about diagnosis
Provide info about wellness self management/caregiver empowerment resources
Educate about the need for a consistent approach
Provide info about typical child/adolescent development

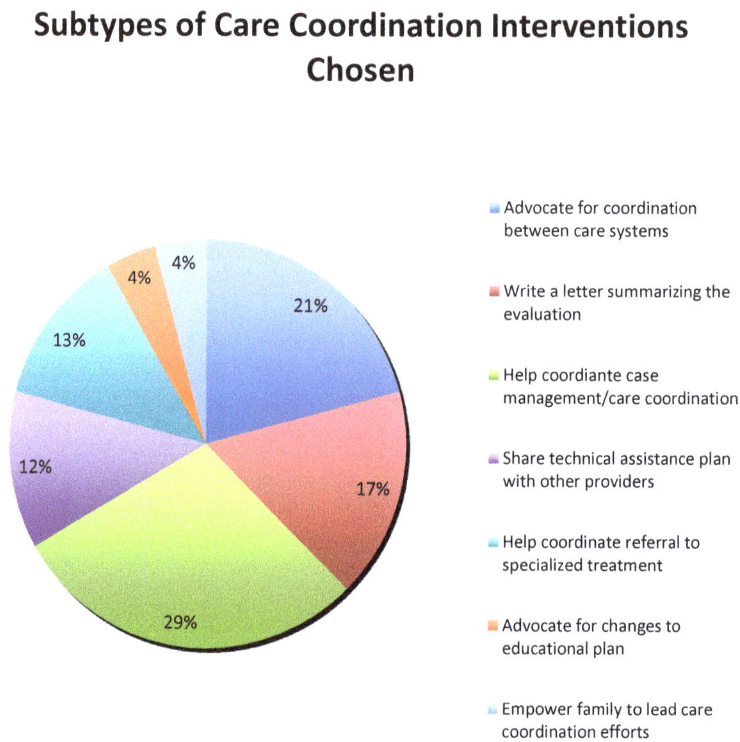
Subtypes of Care Coordination Interventions Chosen
21%
17%
29%
12%
13%
4%
4%
Advocate for coordination between care systems
Write a letter summarizing the evaluation
Help coordiante case management/care coordination
Share technical assistance plan with other providers
Help coordinate referral to specialized treatment
Advocate for changes to educational plan
Empower family to lead care coordination efforts

References

Agius, M. and Butler, S. (2012). Rationale for clinical interventions in prodromal psychosis: Are such interventions safe? *Psychiatria Danubina*, 24 (Suppl. 1), 28-35. Retrieved from http://www.hdbp.org/psychiatria_danubina/pdf/dnb_vol24_sup1/dnb_vol24_sup1_28.pdf .

Anderson, G. and Knickman, J. R. (2001). Changing the chronic care system to meet people's needs. *Health Affairs*, 20, 146-60. doi:10.1377/hlthaff.20.6.146.

Aos, S., Lieb, R., Mayfield, J., Miller, M., and Pennucci, A. (2004). *Benefits and costs of prevention and early intervention programs for youth* (Document no. 04-07-3901). Retrieved from Washington State Institute for Public Policy http://www.wsipp.wa.gov/ReportFile/881/Wsipp_Benefits-and-Costs-of-Prevention-and-Early-Intervention-Programs-for-Youth_Summary-Report.pdf.

Axelson, D., Birmaher, B., Zelazny, J., Kaufman, J., and Gill, M. K. (2009). *K-sads -PL: 2009 working draft*. Retrieved from http://www.psychiatry.pitt.edu/sites/default/files/Documents/assessments/KSADS-PL_2009_working_draft_full.pdf.

Baksheev, G. N., Allott, K., Jackson, H. J., McGorry, P. D., and Killackey, E. (2012). Predictors of vocational recovery among young people with first-episode psychosis: findings from a randomized controlled trial. *Psychiatric Rehabilitation Journal*, 35, 421-27. doi:10.1037/h0094574.

Buchanan, R. W., Kreyenbuhl, J., Kelly, D. L., Noel, J. M., Boggs, D. L., Fischer, B. A., and Keller, W. (2010). The 2009 schizophrenia port psychopharmacological treatment recommendations and summary statements. *Schizophrenia Bulletin*, 36, 71-93. doi:10.1093/schbul/sbp116.

Calkins, M. E., Moore, T. M., Merikangas, K. R., Burstein, M., Satterthwaite, T. D., Bilker, W. B., and Gur, R. E. (2014). The psychosis spectrum in a young U.S. community sample: findings from the Philadelphia Neurodevelopmental Cohort. *World Psychiatry*, 13, 296-305. doi:10.1002/wps.20152.

Cannon, T. D., Cadenhead, K., Cornblatt, B., Woods, S. W., Addington, J., Walker, E., and Heinssen, R. (2008). Prediction of psychosis in youth at high clinical risk: A multisite longitudinal study in North America. *Archives of General Psychiatry*, 65, 28-37. doi:10.1001/archgenpsychiatry.2007.3.

Chang, W. C., Hui, C. L. M., Tang, J. Y. M., Wong, G. H. Y., Chan, S. K. W., Lee, E. H. M., and Chen, E. Y. H. (2013). Impacts of duration of untreated psychosis on cognition and negative symptoms in first-episode schizophrenia: a 3-year prospective follow-up study. *Psychological Medicine*, 43, 1883-1893. doi:10.1017/s0033291712002838.

Corcoran, C., Davidson, L., Sills-Shahar, R., Nickou, C., Malaspina, D., Miller, T., and McGlashan, T. (2003). A qualitative research study of the evolution of symptoms in individuals identified as prodromal to psychosis. *Psychiatric Quarterly*, 74, 313-32. doi:10.1023/a:1026083309607.

Correll, C. U., Hauser, M., Auther, A. M., and Cornblatt, B. A. (2010). Research in people with the psychosis risk syndrome: a review of the current evidence and future directions. *Journal of Child Psychology and Psychiatry*, 51, 390-431. doi:10.1111/j.1469-7610.2010.02235.x.

Croghan, T. W. and Brown, J. D. (2010). *Integrating mental health treatment into the patient centered medical home*. Rockville, MD: Agency for Healthcare Research and Quality.

Dixon, L. B., Dickerson, F., Bellack, A. S., Bennett, M., Dickinson, D., Goldberg, R. W., and Kreyenbuhl, J. (2010). The 2009 schizophrenia port psychosocial treatment recommendations and summary statements. *Schizophrenia Bulletin*, 36, 48-70. doi:10.1093/schbul/sbp115.

Fontanella, C. A., Guada, J., Phillips, G., Ranbom, L., and Fortney, J. C. (2014). Individual and contextual-level factors associated with continuity of care for adults with schizophrenia. *Administration and Policy in Mental Health and Mental Health Services Research*, 41, 572-87. doi:10.1007/s10488-013-0500-x.

Garland, A. F., Kruse, B., and Aarons, G. A. (2003). Clinicians and outcome measurement: What's the use? *Journal of Behavioral Health Services and Research*, 30, 393-405. doi:10.1007/bf02287427.

Gearing, R. E. (2008). Evidence-based family psychoeducational interventions for children and adolescents with psychotic disorders. *Journal of the Canadian Academy of Child and Adolescent Psychiatry*, 17, 2-17. Retrieved from http://www.ncbi.nlm.nih.gov/pmc/articles/PMC2247440/.

Goerke, D. and Sanjiv, K. (2013). Substance Abuse and Psychosis. *Child and Adolescent Psychiatric Clinics of North America, 22*, 643-54. doi:10.1016/j.chc.2013.06.001.

Häfner, H. and an der Heiden, W. (1997). Epidemiology of schizophrenia. *Canadian Journal of Psychiatry, 42*, 139-51. Retrieved from http://ww1.cpa-apc.org:8080/publications/archives/PDF/1997/Mar/hafner.pdf.

Hollis, C. (2009). Child and adolescent onset schizophrenia. *Schizophrenia,* 34-53. Retrieved from http://www.health.am/psy/more/child-and-adolescent-onset-schizophrenia/.

Kopelowicz, A., Liberman, R. P., and Zarate, R. (2006). Recent advances in social skills training for schizophrenia. *Schizophrenia Bulletin*, 32 (suppl. 1), 12-23. doi:10.1093/schbul/sbl023.

Kreyenbuhl, J., Nossel, I. R., and Dixon, L. B. (2009). Disengagement from mental health treatment among individuals with schizophrenia and strategies for facilitating connections to care: a review of the literature. *Schizophrenia Bulletin*, *35*, 696-703. doi:10.1093/schbul/sbp046.

Lachman, A. (2014). New developments in diagnosis and treatment update: Schizophrenia/first episode psychosis in children and adolescents. *Journal of Child and Adolescent Mental Health,* 26, 109-24. doi:10.2989/17280583.2014.924416.

Lieberman, J. A., Dixon, L. B., and Goldman, H. H. (2013). Early detection and intervention in schizophrenia: a new therapeutic model. *JAMA*, 310, 689-90. doi:10.1001/jama.2013.8804.

Liu, C. C. and Demjaha, A. (2013). Antipsychotic interventions in prodromal psychosis. *CNS Drugs*, *27*, 197-205. doi:10.1007/s40263-013-0046-1.

Lucksted, A., McFarlane, W., Downing, D., and Dixon, L. (2012). Recent developments in family psychoeducation as an evidence-based practice. *Journal of Marital and Family Therapy*, 38, 101-21. doi:10.1111/j.1752-0606.2011.00256.x.

Lyons, J. (2011). Child and Adolescent Needs and Strengths: NY [Measurement instrument]. Retrieved from https://canstraining.com/lschmidt/cans-new-york/node/printable-copy-of-the-manual.

Maier, W., Cornblatt, B. A., and Merikangas, K. R. (2003). Transition to schizophrenia and related disorders: toward a taxonomy of risk. *Schizophrenia Bulletin,* 29, 693-701. doi:10.1093/oxfordjournals.schbul.a007039.

McClellan, J. and Stock, S. (2013). Practice parameter for the assesssment and treatment of children and adolescents with schizophrenia. *Journal of the American Academy of Child and Adolescent Psychiatry,* 52, 976–90. doi:10.1016/j.jaac.2013.02.008.

McCrone, P., Singh, S. P., Knapp, M., Smith, J., Clark, M., Shiers, D., and Tiffin, P. A. (2013). The economic impact of early intervention in psychosis services for children and adolescents. *Early intervention in psychiatry*, 7, 368-73. doi:10.1111/eip.12024.

McGlashan, T. H., Walsh, B. C., and Woods, S. W. (2010). Structured Interview for Psychosis-risk Syndromes [Measurement instrument]. New Haven: Yale School of Medicine.

———. (2010). *The psychosis-risk syndrome: handbook for diagnosis and follow-up*. New York: Oxford University Press.

McGorry, P. D. (2012). Truth and reality in early intervention. *Australian and New Zealand Journal of Psychiatry,* 46, 313–16. doi:10.1177/0004867412442172.

Mueser, K. T., Deavers, F., Penn, D. L., and Cassisi, J. E. (2013). Psychosocial treatments for schizophrenia. *Annual Review of Clinical Psychology,* 9, 465-97. doi:10.1146/annurev-clinpsy-050212-185620.

Munson, M. R., Jaccard, J., Smalling, S. E., Kim, H., Werner, J. J., and Scott, L. D., Jr. (2012). Static, dynamic, integrated and contextualized: a framework for understanding mental health service use among young adults. *Social Science and Medicine,* 75, 1441-49. doi:10.1016/j.socscimed.2012.05.039.

National Institute of Mental Health. raise Early Treatment Program. Retrieved from https://raiseetp.org/.

Norcross, J. C. and Wampold, B. E. (2011). Evidence-based therapy relationships: Research conclusions and clinical practices. *Psychotherapy, 48,* 98-102. doi.org/10.1037/a0022161.

Norman, K. R. and Breitborde, N. J. (2014). Collaborative/therapeutic assessment for early psychosis. *Schizophrenia Research,* 154, 122-23. doi:10.1016/j.schres.2014.02.016.

Norman, R. M. G., Scholten, D. J., Malla, A. K., and Ballageer, T. (2005). Early signs in schizophrenia-spectrum disorders. *Journal of Nervous and Mental Disease,* 193, 17-23. doi:10.1097/01.nmd.0000149214.17924.d9.

Osgood, D. W., Foster, E. M., and Courtney, M. E. (2010). Vulnerable populations and the transition to adulthood. *Focus on Children,* 20 (1), 209-29. doi:10.1353/foc.0.0047.

Pescosolido, B. (2011). Organizing the sociological landscape for the next decades of health and health care research: the network episode model III-R as cartographic subfield guide. In B. Pescosolido, J. Martin, J. McLeod, and A. Rogers (eds.), *Handbook of the sociology of health, illness, and healing,* pp. 39-66. New York: Springer.

Piskulic, D., Barbato, M., Liu, L., and Addington, J. (2015). Pilot study of cognitive remediation therapy on cognition in young people at clinical high risk of psychosis. *Psychiatry Research*, 225, 93-98. doi:10.1016/j.psychres.2014.10.021.

Robinson, D. G., Schooler, N. R., John, M., Correll, C. U., Marcy, P., Addington, J., and Kane, J. M. (2015). Prescription practices in the treatment of first-episode schizophrenia spectrum disorders: data from the National raise-ETP study. *American Journal of Psychiatry*, 172, 237-48. doi:10.1176/appi.ajp.2014.13101355.

Shioiri, T., Shinada, K., Kuwabara, H., and Someya, T. (2007). Early prodromal symptoms and diagnoses before first psychotic episode in 219 inpatients with schizophrenia. *Psychiatry and Clinical Neurosciences*, 61, 348-54. doi:10.1111/j.1440-1819.2007.01685.x.

Srihari, V. H., Tek, C. T., Kucukgoncu, S., Phutane, V. H., Breitborde, N. J. K., Pollard, J., and Woods, S. W. (2014). First-episode services for psychotic disorders in the U.S. public sector: a pragmatic randomized controlled trial. *Psychiatric Services*. Advance online publication. doi:10.1176/appi.ps.201400236.

Substance Abuse and Mental Health Services Administration. (2009). *Family psychoeducation: the evidence.* (HHS Publication No. SMA-09-4422). Rockville, MD: Center for Mental Health Services, Substance Abuse and Mental Health Services Administration, U. S. Department of Health and Human Services.

Sullivan, S., Lewis, G., Wiles, N., Thompson, A., and Evans, J. (2013). Psychotic experiences and social functioning: a longitudinal study. *Social Psychiatry and Psychiatric Epidemiology*, 48, 1053-65. doi:10.1007/s00127-013-0715-x.

The Internet Mental Health Initiative (2010). Worldwide early diagnosis and treatment centers for psychosis and schizophrenia.

Retrieved from http://www.schizophrenia.com/earlypsychosis.htm#.

Tolan, P. H. and Dodge, K. A. (2005). Children's mental health as a primary care and concern: a system for comprehensive support and service. *American Psychologist*, 60, 601. doi:10.1037/0003-066X.60.6.601.

van Kampen, D. (2005). Pathways to schizophrenic psychosis: a SISREL-tested model of the unfolding of the schizophrenic prodrome. *Journal of Clinical Psychology*, 61, 909-38. doi:10.1002/jclp.20134.

Winsper, C., Singh, S. P., Marwaha, S., Amos, T., Lester, H., Everard, L., and Birchwood, M. (2013). Pathways to violent behavior during first-episode psychosis: a report from the UK National eden Study. *JAMA Psychiatry*, 70, 1287-93. doi:10.1001/jamapsychiatry.2013.2445.

Winters, N. C. and Metz, W. P. (2009). The wraparound approach in systems of care. *Psychiatric Clinics of North America*, 32, 135-51. doi:10.1016/j.psc.2008.11.007.

Woodberry, K. A., Serur, R. A., Hallinan, S. B., Mesholam-Gately, R. I., Giuliano, A. J., Wojcik, J. D., and Seidman, L. J. (2014). Frequency and pattern of childhood symptom onset reported by first episode schizophrenia and clinical high risk youth. *Schizophrenia Research*, 158, 45-51. doi:10.1016/j.schres.2014.05.017.

Wykes, T., Huddy, V., Cellard, C., McGurk, S. R., and Czobor, P. (2011). A meta-analysis of cognitive remediation for schizophrenia: methodology and effect sizes. *American Journal of Psychiatry*, 168, 472-85. doi:10.1176/appi.ajp.2010.10060855.

www.ingramcontent.com/pod-product-compliance
Lightning Source LLC
LaVergne TN
LVHW051103210926
848486LV00019B/409